HE COULD MAKE WORDS SING

AN ORDINARY MAN DURING EXTRAORDINARY TIMES

DAVID GREENE

ISBN: 978-0-9980182-0-1 (print)
ISBN: 978-0-9980182-1-8 (epub)
ISBN: 978-0-9980182-2-5 (epdf)

Library of Congress Control Number: 2017948580

Printed in the United States of America.

TABLE OF CONTENTS

ORDINARY MEN, A GENERATION APART

After my father enlisted in the army at the outbreak of World War II and America's entry, he was stationed at Fort Bragg in North Carolina. He met Ann Reynolds, a woman with whom he developed a close relationship, so much so that during his time in the European Front they shared love letters. I don't remember when I first learned about his relationship with Ann, but I knew her name before an incident that would give me great insight into how intimate a relationship they had had.

A newspaper reporter in North Carolina had launched a project asking families to submit love letters written by GIs during World War II and sent to family members. Ann responded by submitting my dad's letters and hers—the letters became a chapter in the book that was finally published. My dad's letters were very poignant. When my dad came back from the war after a stint doing administrative work in Germany postwar because he was fluent in German, one would think by the love and passion expressed in those letters that he and Ann would reconnect. This was not a generation in which that sort of thing would easily happen. Ann was Southern and Protestant, my dad a northern Jew. Their union was not to be had. My dad went back to Brooklyn, met my mother and married. Ann met the man who would be her husband, married and raised a family as well. However, the two of them kept in touch throughout their lives.

This by way of prelude: Years later I watched the reaction of my mother and my father when I brought home for the first time the woman whom I would a year later marry—an Episcopalian from Kentucky who had fallen in love with this northern Jew. What touched me most about that first meeting, the introduction of Randolph to my parents, is how cold and almost cruel my mother was toward Randolph—and *how warmly my father greeted her. How adroitly he handled the many awkward moments when my mother exclaimed, "Randolph, what kind of name is that for a woman?" to which my father said, "May we call you Kentuck?"*

I don't know if he knew how deeply that touched Randolph, but it was clear that a bond had been created. A bond that was only cemented further when my family came to Hamilton to see Randolph in a Chekov play. She had a leading role. I don't think I saw much of the play because I spent much of it watching my father and not the stage.

If there was anyone who looked more radiant than Randolph on stage as the femme fatale, it was my father. I thought he had fallen in love with her because he had a love for theatre. He had fallen in love not only with a marvelous actress but with the idea that his son would do what he could not a generation before—consummating a relationship with a woman so different from himself. It did not hurt that Randolph was a terrific athlete and tennis player.

I was my father a generation later: a northern Jew permitted to pursue a romance with a Southern gentile.

—Richard Greissman

Who was that Northern Jew who came so close to marrying a Protestant Southern belle? Harry Greissman, as all of us are, was unique in some respects, representative in others. Something about him touched her. Although Anne first liked another GI named Harry more, she preferred Harry Greissman, the one who, she said, *"could make words sing."*

Like many men of his era, he was a product of his experiences, and as many were, he was sometimes underappreciated as a professional, husband, and father. No matter how uniquely talented, brilliant, giving in his own way, or how high he flew, he was often in the shadow of others, sometimes at home.

A son of poor immigrant Austrian Jews, he was talented enough to be a newspaperman in high school, in college, and in the army. He had always said he wanted to be a sportswriter and always talked about writing a novel. He was certainly talented enough. Yet he didn't. The dream could wait. Forever. Instead, following his years in the army, and a short stint as a reporter, he married, became an "ad man" in a grey flannel suit with a more guaranteed income for a man of his generation, whose destiny like so many others was to be the provider, the breadwinner, the foundation of family life during the 1950s and 1960s.

Yet he was, after all, a member of the "Silent Generation." He went to all four years of high school during the height of the Depression. A college star, he was a hero during World War II. In an anti-Semitic advertising world, he rose in the ranks and was well respected.

Harry was fifty-seven when I met him. Although there were times when I was his *All in the Family* "Meathead" to his "Archie," we generally got along very well. He helped me with tennis and writing. We occasionally watched sports on TV. Of course we spent holidays together with family. He was most kind and loving to my mom who was two years his elder. As members of that generation they shared many memories of their troubled lives as kids and young adults. They understood each other's heartaches and disappointments in life.

To me, though, he looked sad as he often faded into the background. Harry sat in his chair, read, played tennis, and told bad puns. I vowed never to become Harry. As his daughter Jamie said, "He seemed to accept it, and didn't mind it much, or he just didn't complain. He was not a complainer. He just did what he had to do." I learned of his skills, his intellect, his poetry, and his complex relationships with people. At the same time, I became more aware of how he was but one of the millions of prideful untold lives of the men of his generation, so often overlooked as they aged.

He was loved, and praised as a father, yet I believe he yearned for more self-satisfaction. He was extremely proud of all three of his children's achievements: Richard became the highest ranked non-Ph.D. staff member at the University of Kentucky. Jamie earned a Ph.D. in psychology and has been a practicing psychologist for thirty-six years. Allan has become one of the leading pediatric intensive care physicians in the country. In researching this work, I found Richard was his inspiration and muse. Jamie had far fewer memories of Harry, and Allan still labors over guilt about their relationship.

Why did Harry and others like him choose that path? Was it their nature? What environmental factors contributed to those decisions at work and at home? We can only guess. Certainly, we are all creatures who have to face various biases and ceilings during our lifetimes. Some of us, even of the same generation, never stop fighting. Others give up, acquiesce, and try to live for another day. Why do some flower and some barely bud?

What was in Harry's personality that restricted his full flowering, whether at work or at home? Perhaps William Wordsworth said it best in his poem, *"My Heart Leaps Up When I Behold,"*

> *My heart leaps up when I behold*
> *A rainbow in the sky:*
> *So was it when my life began;*
> *So is it now I am a man;*
> *So be it when I shall grow old,*
> *Or let me die!*
> *The Child is father of the Man;*
> *And I could wish my days to be*
> *Bound each to each by natural piety.*

The phrase "The Child is father of the Man" has become famous in its own right. Meaning who we are and how we act as adults is dependent very much on who we were and how we acted as children; it is the basis for a great deal of psychotherapy.

Perhaps here lies the answer. Harry was given two paradoxical traits as a child of his times and of his parents. One, as a young American, was the freedom to learn and explore ideas, language, knowledge, and creativity in which he thrived. The other was the imprisonment and restrictions imposed on him by strict immigrant parents, an even more strict religious upbringing, the Depression, the army and the war in which he bravely fought. These paradoxes are not unlike many Americans have faced then and now.

Harry wanted to behold more rainbows. His heart leapt whenever it did. His intellect sought to fly, and often it did when he created at work, with his brother Lou, or with his eldest son, Richard, who shared many of Harry's traits. In those regards he was like so many men of his Greatest Generation. They were all children of the Depression, scraping to get by and developing what was commonly called a "Depression mentality." They sacrificed risk for security and spending for saving.

EXTRAORDINARY CIRCUMSTANCES

"There are no extraordinary men . . . just extraordinary circumstances that ordinary men are forced to deal with."

—William Halsey

For however "Great" Harry's generation was, a term coined by Tom Brokaw in his book *The Greatest Generation*, their formative years were filled with a great deal of angst. Maybe that is what made them great. During the Great Depression, as Brokaw points out, "Despair hovered over the land like a plague. They had watched their parents lose their businesses, their farms, their jobs, and their hopes. They had learned to accept a future that played out one day." (xix-xx)

Many of these men were sons and grandsons of immigrants who fled foreign famine, tyranny, revolution, racism, and anti-Semitism. Whether Italian, Irish, Japanese, Chinese, Latin American, or Eastern European, they had all faced discrimination and grew up trying to assimilate and become true Americans. They were shaped by their experiences here, yet they carried their traditional cultural baggage with them throughout their lives.

During World War II, many died for their beloved country, of which they tried so hard to be a part. None returned unscathed from battle. All came home different men than who they were when they left for war. They had to leave home, be stationed stateside in places quite different from their hometowns, and fight overseas. Relationships with family and friends at home changed. New relationships with fellow soldiers were built and then lost. Even flourishing romantic relationships perished like cut flowers.

They were the "Silent" or "Traditionalist" generation that sought financial security. They were primarily patient conformists, and team players with traditional family values.

They were loyal to their employers and expected the same in return. They thought promotions, raises, and recognition came from job tenure. Often, they were disappointed.

And, especially in the case of war veterans, they were often silent, with horrid images to be forgotten. Halsey's words can probably describe many of our fathers and grandfathers of that generation. Silent, ordinary men, they did not want to remember their most extraordinary moments. Harry was simply one of millions, as are we all.

The most significant circumstance men of Harry's generation went through had to be their service during World War II, and the apprehension that preceded it. In a January 31, 1941, letter, Harry tells his oldest brother Jack that, in retrospect, he is happy he never sent him a "lost" letter because it was full of

> *a few choice diatribes on the matter of the draft—I had just received a notice that I was classified 1A [fit for service] in the draft, call no. 196, which meant I would be called in February.*

He continues:

> *Thanks, however to that salivary [Only Harry could use that as an adjective.] oratory which has been a plague as well as often as a blessing, I talked my way into indefinite deferment, not so much on the strength or weakness of my bad arm (out here they are calling men with missing fingers to the colors) as on my willingness to serve as soon as matters at home are straightened out—to wit, Sol's call and Abe's unemployment.*
>
> *Too bad about Sol though, although on further thought, maybe it is better to get it over with now, when things are so uncertain, than later when he might be hauled from an important job. No matter how one looks at it, it's all a rotten business—but as usual, one must make the best of it.*

Showing off his multi-linguistic skills, he continues:

> *Comme por moi . . . I've really refined into a decent ad man and have gathered a few more feathers for the family cap. My latest promotion—which caught our competitors napping—gave us the biggest days we had since x-mas in last week's Thurs-Fri-Sat campaign. Sat.—which had the pressure of heavy newspaper and radio ads behind it was the biggest, most profitable day since our opening, and this is usually the deadest part of the year for our type of trade. . . . Hammond is now open 10 weeks and we are now taking in about $3,000 a week—fair enough?*

That deferment didn't last too long. He would soon be separated from family in Brooklyn, New York, and work buddies in the Chicago area. The next time Jack and the family heard from Harry, he would be Private Harry Greissman, 320855522 T41, assigned to T.R. 902, Battery D, 3rd Battalion, 1st FA Tng Regiment, FARTC, stationed at "beautiful" Fort Bragg, North Carolina.

Just like that, similar to so many others of his generation, his life vanished. His life and stories would now center on life in the Army and would until his discharge five years later in 1946. How many men return unchanged form a five-year stint in the military, even without the warfare? Harry certainly would become a changed man, a very changed man from the prewar young man with literary dreams.

He became one of the millions of veterans who suffered the "slings and arrows of outrageous fortune." They came home wounded, maimed, or simply returned as emotional shells of their former selves listening only to their individual "Sounds of Silence."

They survived immigrant poverty, the Depression, and risked their lives in World War II for the freedom to create a safe and secure world for their children. Many, like Harry, eventually shrank from taking chances and fulfilling dreams of younger years. They, like Harry, lived in the shadow of what they could have been.

He could make words sing, but was it enough for him? The treasure trove of evidence from his work at the end of World War II as a military interpreter as well as his work as an "ad man" that he saved indicates he felt pride in his accomplishments, except for the book he never wrote. Maybe this book can vindicate him and other ordinary men like him.

The bottom tag listed next of kin to be notified. Note that it is his closest brother Louis, not his parents.

BACK TO THE FUTURE

To what extent does nurturing by events play a role in our futures? The post-9/11 children of the twenty-first century know a very different world shaped by that day. Will the results of the 2016 election create circumstances that will further shape their adult lives? Will the children of poor working-class Latin or Middle Eastern immigrant families living in Los Angeles, Chicago, or New York be shaped by policies created in a Trump administration? How will a generation that was raised through the Great Recession and threat of impending terrorism be shaped by the current administration?

Were these types of questions asked one hundred years ago when Harry Greissman entered the world and grew up as an Orthodox Jew in a poor working-class neighborhood in Brooklyn? To what extent did anti-Semitism affect him? How was World War I going to change his childhood? To what extent did growing up as a street kid in Brooklyn and going to high school during the Depression make him who he and others became?

Muslim Ban! No More Refugees! Keep the Islamic Terrorists out! Make America Great Again. These 2017 slogans and executive policy plans are not new. The history of American immigration is dotted with anti-alien ideas and acts. When the Irish came to the United States during the Great Famine as refugees from hunger, the response here was horrible. They were depicted as apes, Africans, murderers, drunks, cheats, agitators, even part of an alleged "voter fraud" operation.

http://www.victoriana.com/history/irish-political-cartoons.html

Fifty years later, in 1892, the Chinese were actually "excluded" by the Chinese Exclusion Act that prohibited all immigration of Chinese laborers who were "taking jobs" from Americans. However, it was the Irish and Chinese who actually helped "Make America Great Again" by being the primary labor forces in the building of the transcontinental railroad.

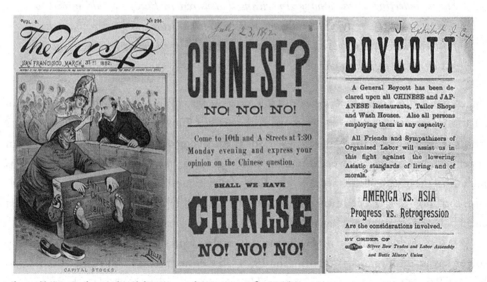

http://www.irehr.org/tag/chinese-exclusion-act-of-1882/

World War I brought on a new wave of anti-immigration sentiment as depicted by this 1917 cartoon. It appeared to be based on religion as well as nationality.

https://www.nytimes.com/2017/03/15/arts/design/1917-exhibit-world-war-i-jewish-immigration.html

The war and the revolution resulted in strict limits on immigration to the United States, reflecting a fear among Americans that unrest in Europe would spread to their country. The restrictions were not overtly aimed at Jews, but because the quotas from countries with high Jewish populations were tightened, fewer Jews were able to settle in the United States.[1]

Eugenics was the pseudoscience whose sole purpose was to improve the genetic quality of a nation's or state's population. How many Americans know that it was practiced decades before it was used by the Nazis to weed out those deemed "undesirable"? The American eugenics movement received extensive funding from various corporate foundations including the Carnegie Institution, the Rockefeller Foundation, and the Harriman rail-road fortune.[2] In fact, the Immigration Acts of 1921 and 1924 that set quotas were almost entirely based on the lobbying efforts of the supporters of the eugenics movement.

It was in this ordinary national atmosphere that Harry Greissman, a rather ordinary son of Jewish immigrants, was born. The 1920 US Census has his birth year as 1916. Who knows? Records were not very accurate. He was one of thirteen children born to Austrian Orthodox Jewish immigrants, Aaron and Mary Greissman of 105 South 3rd Street, Williamsburg, Brooklyn, New York. He was one of "them." How would Harry and hundreds of thousands of others survive—no, thrive—in this atmosphere?

Harry grew up in a typical Jewish immigrant family with a dad and mom who worked in the garment trade and their older aspirational offspring upgrading their occupations to something more business based. Aaron came to America in 1890 and was naturalized in December 1901 while working as a tailor. No surprises there. He was a typical Jewish immigrant, down to the occupation.

Our seemingly regular history of bigotry and racism surfaces even on an official US form used ONLY for "Person claiming citizenship through naturalization of Husband or Parent." It seems eugenics was important in judging whether those people could get a passport at the turn of the twentieth century. This official form describes Mary as born in Austria (then the Austro-Hungarian Empire) and therefore suspect, eugenically speaking.

AGE: 24 years   MOUTH: medium
STATURE 5'6"   CHIN: medium
FOREHEAD: broad   HAIR: Black
EYES: black   COMPLEXION: light
NOSE: medium   FACE: oval

According to Harry's cousin, Susan Beaudry,

> *Uncle Harry once mentioned his mother to me and I can remember him telling me she was from Vienna. The way he told it, it sounded like she was a princess. I wish I had asked more questions about where she came from and how she got here. When they were growing up I know they were very poor. My mother told me they grew up in a rough neighborhood. From what I gathered Aaron Greissman, my grandfather, was a tailor but didn't work much. My grandmother, Mary, took in laundry. Now with eight to ten children it sounded like most of their income came from her. My mother told me that my grandfather spent all his time in shul.*

As many other Jewish immigrants before them, they may have traversed the "Jews' Highway," east on Delancey and across the Williamsburg Bridge[3] to Williamsburg, Brooklyn, and eventually to the now heavily Hasidic Borough Park section of Brooklyn.

Growing up an Orthodox Jew made one different. The obvious differences were keeping a kosher home with all the rules (no meat and dairy, Sabbath/holiday plates different from regular dishes, no pork or bacon), or walking to synagogue regularly on Saturdays in sneakers. Yet many Jewish secular values were American. For example, social justice, political involvement to better lives for all, and creating a world free from injustice were all part of the "American Dream." So were upward social mobility, unionism, socialism, education, and hard work. Did that matter to Harry's Christian neighbors?

The difficulty of adult immigrants in parting with the ways of the old country, in learning to read English and speak it without an accent, in finding gainful employment, and in general, mastering the new environment, in many cases led to the reversal of roles between parents and children. Young children learned English more readily, and it was not uncommon for them to serve as family spokespersons when dealing with teachers, principals, policemen, and other non-Jewish authorities.

Inevitably, many children, feeling more American than their parents, were embarrassed by the latter's foreignness and derided them for being "greenhorns"—and then often felt guilty for it.[4] As a result, many American-born children of Orthodox immigrants did what many kids still do—they questioned and rebelled.

Here was most felt the influence of Americanization. Americanization also meant fitting in, not being different; not dressing as if you came from a *shtetl* (a small Jewish town or village in eastern Europe); losing the Yiddish accent. It included doing American things that violated ancient customs and traditions like going to Saturday Dodgers games or staying out late with your friends and dressing hip. How much did all this matter to "real Americans"?

None of the Greissman children seemed religious. They all identified with being Jewish culturally. Many, like them, "desperately did not want to be like their parents," says Maurice Sendak. "We wanted to be American. So there were the Movies. There was Mickey Mouse, King Kong, Fred Astaire to nourish our fantasies ..."[5] Even the idea of going to college was a rebellious way to become American. The brightest went to secular college instead of Torah study. Exploring creativity and talents became more important than following rituals and being stuck in the past.

It even meant placing country over ethnicity. Becoming a Jewish-American to many was more important than staying an American Jew. The use of English was a key indicator of how far one came. To be fluent, with no trace of accent, was to belong. To be fluid with the pen or typewriter was to belong even more so. Harry was fluid to the nth degree. Although he became fluent in French, Spanish, Italian, German, Yiddish, English, and Hebrew, he sounded and wrote as if his ancestors stepped off the Mayflower. By the time Harry went to college he had become a secular Jew whose family practiced so-called domestic rituals such as Friday night candles, keeping Kosher, and observing the holidays.

Yo, I'm From Brooklyn Too

Brooklyn is a world unto itself. It even has its own version of English. Only Brooklynites can define Brooklyn as Larry King did, "When you are from Brooklyn, everything, else is Tokyo." I have no idea what he meant, but that's the point. Being raised in the Bronx, as I was, I knew two things about Brooklyn, that it was in many ways similar to the Bronx, but in one big way different and hated: It was Brooklyn.

Harry grew up in what appeared to be an ethnically mixed, polyglot Brooklyn neighborhood. What was it like growing up as a son of Orthodox Jews in a neighborhood like that? There were some who were open-minded but not many. Thugs beat up on Jewish kids. Some Jewish kids learned how not to be bullied and in turn had to become neighborhood toughs, or at least they had to be tough outside the neighborhood. My dad, who was born the same year as Harry, tells stories of his childhood growing up in East Harlem and the Bronx as a Jew having to either run or fight his way through the Irish and Italian neighborhoods between his house and either school or other destinations. I imagine it was the same for Harry.

Both outer boroughs were and still are filled with bustling ethnic neighborhoods that bordered other bustling ethnic neighborhoods. As such they were very much like small towns. Sometimes those in the next "town" were like you and friendly, but other times they were not like you and their "towns" became dangerous places to go. Mothers would hang out the window, "watching, always watching" just as Mother Sister did in Spike Lee's *Do the Right Thing*, which depicted the then Black neighborhood of Bedford Stuyvesant in the mid-1980s.

Harry's neighborhoods were filled with German and Austrian Jews. Adjoining neighborhoods, however, were filled with gentile German/Austrian Americans. During the 1930s a rather large number of Nazi sympathizers appeared in several Brooklyn neighborhoods.

For example, when Harry was in college, "On November 17 and 18, 1934, a gathering of 'Friends of the New Germany' aka Nazis, drawn from all over the Eastern U.S., met in Brooklyn."[6] On August 12, 1935, the *New York World Telegram* reported that there were 1,100 Nazis in Ridgewood, Brooklyn. Why? How could they sympathize with a racist, anti-Semitic national leader?

Although a world apart, kids in Brooklyn and kids in the Bronx grew up similarly, hanging on stoops (apartment building steps to the uninitiated), played street games like stickball, skully, Johnny on the pony, or stoopball. We ate the same kind of foods like hot dogs, pizza, and pastrami sandwiches, washed down by the ubiquitous egg cream. Whether in Brooklyn or the Bronx, kids would go to the candy store where they could get ice cream or the best drink ever invented: the chocolate egg cream. The chocolate egg cream was part seltzer, part milk, and part U-Bet chocolate syrup. No other syrup would do. Any other syrup was imitation. So whether on the stoop, or the corner, the boys and girls of Brooklyn and the Bronx grew up very similarly except they were from Brooklyn, a Long Island borough, and we were on the mainland.

The movies shared their version of Brooklyn guys, usually swarthy Italian or Jewish guys in movies about World War II. In fact, 326,000 Brooklyn males (58 percent of ages 18–37) served. Those images would do a lot to create stereotypes that might be hard to overcome. How much were those stereotypes based on fact? How much is any stereotype based on fact?

THIS CAN'T BE
HAPPENING IN AMERICA

New York City was one of the hardest hit areas of the country during the Great Depression. By March 1930, there were fifty bread lines on the Lower East Side alone, serving 50,000 meals a day to the hungry. By 1932, half of New York's manufacturing plants were closed, one in every three New Yorkers was unemployed, and roughly 1.6 million were on some form of relief. The city was unprepared to deal with this crisis. Vacancy rates nearly doubled as the number of people with money to pay rent plummeted.[7]

In 1932, we lived in a two-family house in Flatbush, Brooklyn. I remember seeing well-dressed men on bread lines, selling apples on the corner of Canal and Broadway in Manhattan, near where my father had a factory. He owned a chemical company, and had to let his employees go—both the workers and the salesmen. He would go out during the day to try to get orders for his plumbing and heating products and come back with one worker. They'd work most of the night on the third floor of the walk-up to package the chemicals.

I remember my mother walking down 24th Street in Flatbush, collecting clothing and shoes for a refugee family. [And I remember] I was going to have a birthday and my mother said, "Don't expect any presents, because the banks have closed." It scarred me for life.

—Rhoda Fidler[8]

I have vivid memories of seeing people's possessions carried out of their homes and deposited on the curb, and usually without terrible preparation. The Sheriff would appear and say "you're evicted" and there was no time to pack. So you would have a tearful scene, with people sitting on the sidewalk amidst their belongings.

> *It was a practice for people to go around the neighborhood and ring doorbells and say "we've been thrown out of our house," and collect a dollar here, a dollar there, whatever people could give, and get themselves moved back in again.*[9]

That was the world Harry grew up in while he was a teenager. Although upward mobility was an important part of being a Jewish immigrant family in New York City, how was that to happen under these circumstances?

Even though the country was in the midst of the Great Depression, Harry's siblings sacrificed and worked so he could be the first in his family to go to college. By April 1932, when Harry was still in high school, more than 750,000 people in New York were on a form of welfare. Another 160,000 were on the waiting list to get relief funds. But Harry was lucky enough to go to college.

Between the stock market crash of October 24,1929, and the time Harry graduated college in 1937, the Great Depression had already taken its toll on millions of Americans. By 1933, when the Great Depression reached its peak and Franklin Delano Roosevelt had been sworn in as our new president, 13 to 15 million Americans (approximately 25 percent) were unemployed and nearly half of the country's banks had failed. Panic was everywhere.

During the Roaring Twenties the stock market had become the new "Big Thing." Average Americans saw it as an easy way to make money and move up that slippery social mobility ladder. "Why not me?" So, as seems to still be the case, Wall Street and banks found a way to make money from those dreams. Anyone could now buy stock with as little as 10 percent of its value, "on margin," borrowing the difference from a bank or broker. Of course the banks and brokers charged interest, and all loans had to be repaid. That was easy money for all, provided the market kept going up. Not only were brokers, banks, and investors reaping profits, the entire US economy depended on the booming market. If this sounds all too familiar, please just take a deep breath and continue.

Wishing and hoping for wealth and success often breeds blindness to obvious warning signs. As more people bought stocks with borrowed money, the demand for stocks increased—as did the prices. In 1928 alone, the stock market's value doubled. "No risk, no reward" became the mantra.

President Coolidge was quoted as saying, "The business of America is business."[10] During the presidential campaign of 1928, President Hoover promised voters "a chicken in every pot and two cars in every garage." Life was going to be "the cat's meow," an archaic slang term that in various contexts meant "excellent," "stylish," or "impressive to the ladies." Oh, were they wrong.

Finally, the days of reckoning came. Between October 24 and October 29 (Black Thursday and Tuesday respectively), approximately 29 million shares of stock were sold in a panic. Investors tried to recoup their money by selling their stocks, which were becoming more worthless by the day. That, in turn, lowered the values of stocks even more. Everyone lost.

Investors were forced to pay back the 90 percent margin loans with money they didn't have. When people couldn't pay back those loans, many banks were forced to close and could not pay back their depositors. As people lost confidence in their banks, they demanded their money. The banks could not even give savers their deposits because they had only a "margin" of cash reserves. The rest was out in unpaid "margin" loans. So, they had to call in more loans ... and the dominos continued to fall until more and more banks failed. Even those who never invested in the market and who thought they had kept their money in a "safe" bank were now bankrupt.

What is it with that word, *margin*? Maybe we should stop using it.

The results were huge drops in consumer spending and investment. Factories and other businesses fired their workers. For those who were lucky enough to remain employed, wages fell and buying power decreased. Unemployment rose daily. By 1930, 4 million Americans were out of work. By 1931 that number had risen to 6 million. Bread lines, soup kitchens and rising numbers of homeless people became more and more common in America's towns and cities. Shantytowns, soon renamed "Hoovervilles," popped up everywhere, even in Central Park. There were no homeless shelters.

"Hoover flags" were empty pants pockets turned inside out.

As the saying went ...

> *Hoover was the Engineer*
> *Mellon rang the bell*
> *Wall Street gave the signal*
> *Then the country went to Hell.*[11]

http://chiseler.org/post/22524370633/
hoover-flags

http://allday.com/post/293-timeless-photos-of-
new-york-city-during-the-crash-and-the-great-
depression/

From Immigrant Boy to Depression Era Man

Harry was a January New Utrecht High School graduate in 1932. He is listed as number 14 on this page in his high school yearbook, *The Comet*. He was one of 624

graduates. One of the fictional stories in the yearbook, titled "Class Prophecy" talks about a classmate's future 1952 play, *Green Galoshes*, starring two other classmates. The story then goes on to say, "And Harry Greissman is the publicity agent." WHAT? How did they know that in 1952 Harry would be an ad man? Talk about prophecy!

Harry also made it on to a page celebrating "Utrecht's' '32's thirty-two." Here he "answers to Harry" and "should be taller." It seems his "worst crime" was "NUHS-mongering"; he was "famous for" his "virtue"; his "weakness" was "ice cream and cake." He must have really loved words even in high school because he is front and center in a picture of the "English book room squad" and the *NUHS* staff. I gather *NUHS*, notably not N.U.H.S., was the high school paper.

In the directory, Harry "small but snappy" Greissman was supposed to go to NYU. He didn't.

Few children of immigrants went to college. It seems he couldn't afford it. That's where the prophecy of NYU fell through. However, in February 1933, because of the sacrifice of his family, Harry was one of the "exactly two hundred and sixty eight bewildered, but sometimes optimistic lower freshmen"[12] at The School of Business and Civic Administration of the City College of New York. Here he earned his Bachelor of Business Administration degree.

Harry entered college before Franklin Delano Roosevelt took office, at the height of the Depression. How could they afford not only to lose an income but also pay for college? His family decided it was more important for him to go to school than work. The whole family sacrificed. His older siblings worked so their younger and gifted brother could reach his potential.

How privileged was he to live in New York City, which had free public higher education? Many of today's poor and middle-class children of immigrants wish they had that advantage. How lucky was he that he came from a family that would not let him NOT go to college?

Maybe it was Roosevelt's optimism. Harry actually entered college before FDR's March 4 inauguration speech. The 20th Amendment changed inauguration day to January 20, but that wouldn't take effect until 1937. They hadn't yet heard FDR say, "The only thing we have to fear ... is fear itself." He hadn't yet created a four-day "bank holiday" during which all banks would close so that Congress could pass reform legislation and reopen those banks determined to be sound. He hadn't yet passed legislation to stabilize industrial and agricultural production, create jobs, and stimulate recovery. He hadn't yet created the Federal Deposit Insurance Corporation (FDIC) to protect depositors' accounts and the Securities and Exchange Commission (SEC) to regulate the stock market and prevent abuses of the kind that led to the 1929 crash. He hadn't yet created the Tennessee Valley Authority (TVA), which built dams and hydroelectric projects to control flooding and provide electric power to the impoverished Tennessee Valley region of the South, nor the Works Project Administration (WPA), a jobs program that employed 8.5 million people from 1935 to 1943. That was how you "Make America Great Again."

But off to college Harry went. Growing up a Jewish immigrant in New York gave one a strong boost up the social mobility ladder that many immigrants in other parts of the nation did not have. Public schools from kindergarten to graduate school were created and supported to ensure that mobility.

> *Dating to the founding of the Free Academy in 1847, the predecessor of The City College of NY, free tuition had been held as a sacrosanct tradition that had permitted poor high-achieving students to earn diplomas free of charge from the legendary "Harvard of the Proletariat"—City College—and the other public colleges founded during the early 20th century to serve a surging population fueled by immigration.*
>
> *Lawyer Gustave Rosenberg, chairman of the Board of Higher Education, invoked its historic mission: "that in a democratic society, the higher reaches of education are not the exclusive privilege of an elite, but an opportunity and a necessity for all qualified citizens who desire it, regardless of race, creed, or color."[13]*

As the city's population, fueled by immigration, exploded during the early twentieth century, more public colleges were founded to meet the demand for affordable higher education. As train lines were laid out and farmland gave way to neighborhoods, public universities were built throughout the boroughs to keep pace with the city's population growth. By 1930, 36,249 students were in the city's public-college system. That is how you build infrastructure, and improve college education.

In the post–World War I era, discrimination against Jews was common at Ivy League universities and other private educational institutions. Most New York Jewish students and academics had to find their intellectual home at New York City's public colleges, "where ethnicity, religion and national background barred no one." These public colleges were filled with sons and daughters of the poor and middle classes who looked at the world through different lenses than many of their Ivy League colleagues.

> *At City College, the "Harvard of the Proletariat," political movements were hotly debated in its hall during the 1930s. Student activism also surfaced during the Depression era; antiwar groups formed and rallies drew isolationists and idealists. But as European fascism emerged, antiwar sentiment ebbed.[14]*

Harry was in college as the nation pulled its way out of the Depression. As a typical City College student, he commuted to and from school. He attended college in the brand new skyscraping building, School of Business and Civic Administration of the City College of New York, built in 1928. At the dedication ceremony, Dr. Frederick B. Robinson, president of the college, stated the school's mission.

> *The school will seek to produce not merely technicians who can perform their tasks up to the best standards of current practice, but also scholars, who, being broadly cultivated, will see their work in relation to humanity.*
>
> *The industrial world is constantly changing and its technology becomes increasingly complicated. It needs the scholar in action. The chief characteristic of the*

> *scholar is his unending search for truth as it is, from time to time, revealed to the*
> *researcher. The scholar is also impatient of any performance below the standard of*
> *the best that is known. Organized business and our government bureaus and offices*
> *need competent, leaders, lieutenants and craftsmen who are also scholars.*[15]

That was Harry Greissman. According to his yearbook, Harry was the sports editor, managing editor, executive editor, and editor in chief of *The Ticker*, the college's student newspaper, and he was a member of the City College tennis team. Where did a son of Jewish immigrants learn to play the bourgeois game of tennis?

According to Fordham Professor Mark Naison, a Brooklyn street kid and avid tennis player, it seems there were several places. Naison, now 70, "learned tennis at a social democratic bungalow colony", "a summer camp in Massachusetts" and "started taking tennis lessons from a mailman at Lincoln Terrace Park named Phil Rubell. At least 20 of the kids who took lessons from him, for 3 dollars and hour, went on to play Division 1 college tennis. Lincoln Terrace was a Jewish/West Indian tennis enclave in working class middle class Brooklyn. It could have been that way well before I got there in the late 50s." In addition, there was "the relationship between tennis, handball, and paddle ball. There was a huge handball and paddleball scene in Brighton Beach. A lot of the best players in the country came out of those courts. Some of those guys also played tennis."

Scholar. Writer. Athlete. Leader. Harry was all those. He was named "Best Writer" in the yearbook's Senior Celebs section. "Harry Greissman wrote copy for The Lexicon and not one word had to be rewritten … No wonder he was chosen as best writer in his class."

Wait? Did he write that too?

On top of that he was a member of Chi Sigma Mu, a fraternal organization

> *comprised solely of those students [of the college] who have been awarded insignia*
> *of the Student Council. Each semester the honor is conferred upon those members*
> *of the senior class who, in their four years of college, have been outstanding both in*
> *character and in service to the College, as manifested by superior merit and unusual*
> *prominence in the field of extra-curricular activities.*[16]

So, who were these young, scholarly future business leaders? What did they believe? *The Lexicon* created a page called "Senior Opinions." Here are excerpts.

- *They were overwhelmingly sympathetic to the New Deal.*
- *Fifty-one said they were Democrats, nineteen were "non-partisan," eight were socialist, seven communist, and only three Republican. This was in a school of Business!*
- *Seventy-five felt social reform could be accomplished within the framework of the existing social order.*
- *Education was the most effective peace medium.*

- *They were split on war issues. Forty-eight would and forty-one wouldn't sign the Oxford Pledge (the name commonly given to a resolution carried by students of the Oxford debating Union that "this House will in no circumstances fight for its King and Country").*

- *Albert Einstein was their most admired man alive.*

- *Their favorite writers were Edna St. Vincent Millay, Sinclair Lewis, and Eugene O'Neill.*

- *Their favorite actors and actresses were Charles Laughton, Leslie Howard, Myrna Loy, and Helen Hayes.*

- *Their favorite movie of all time was* All Quiet on the Western Front.

- *Their favorite music composers and musicians were Beethoven, Jerome Kern, the NY Philharmonic, and Benny Goodman while their favorite comedy radio actor was Jack Benny.*

- *They read the* New York Times *in the morning and the* NY Post *in the afternoon. The* Post *was a far more liberal newspaper back then. (Yes, there were morning and afternoon newspapers back then.) And their favorite magazines were* The Reader's Digest *and* Esquire.

- *When asked if their college career was a success, 98 said yes educationally while 68 said yes socially. (I guess those long commutes took a toll.)*

- *Future careers? Accounting: 62. Teaching: 24. Advertising: 14 (Harry was one).*

- *Believe in coed colleges? Yes: 118–8. So why was social life bad?*

- *Would you marry for money? No: 60 while 57 said yes.. If so for how much? $60,000. (In 2017 dollars that would be $1,042,361.70.)*

Then they graduated into the real world. That world was preparing for war.

"The World Turned Upside Down"

What was it like to be a young adult then? In many ways it was like growing up now, but much worse. Today, post–Great Recession young adults live in a nation that, depending on where you live, either offers great opportunities, or huge challenges. They face a world at war in the Middle East, threats of terror globally, "Brexit," a highly militarized North Korea, and a world where climate change is threatening us all.

As a young man brought up during the Depression, Harry, like so many others of his era, his dreams dashed, felt he had to take any job. Opportunities were few and far between. What did their futures look like? As they worried about their families' personal futures, they had to become even more concerned about events in Europe and Asia, as forces beyond their control would soon change their optimism. Slowly but surely, militarism, fascism, and Nazism were overcoming fledgling democracies in Japan, Italy, and Germany. The Soviet Union was becoming a dictatorship and by no means one "of the Proletariat."

That same depression scarred the entire world. Whereas the US traditions and its 140-year democratic history enabled it to survive in tact as a democracy, Japan, Italy, and Germany, whose democratic forms of government replaced long-standing monarchies in 1918 as a result of the devastating "Great War" and the "insulting" Treaty of Versailles, were not as fortunate. As a result, neither was the rest of the world, including bright, young, optimistic college students like Harry Greissman. A second World War would be the result. The college graduates of 1937 had to know and fear these events. They were in their early twenties, starting families and jobs, and looking forward to a post–Depression future.

The coming World War would drastically change their lives. How much bias and anti-Semitism did he and other American Jews face as a result of rising Nazi sympathies? Blacks faced struggled with a racist past, present and future. How much did he and his fellow graduates worry about the fate of the world, and thus their lives, and the lives of their families' present and future? How would Harry's fluency in many languages, especially German eventually shape his roles during World War II?

The United States was a democratic republic with the most democratic constitution in the world. It was who we were. We hated the idea of autocratic tyrants like King George ruling over a free people. Unlike European nations, the United States had come out of World War I far better off than we were before it. We gained status and economic clout. We became a world power.

Such was not the case in Japan, Italy, and Germany who all suffered greatly as a result of both World War I and the Depression. To understand the rise of totalitarian governments in Italy, Japan, and Germany, we must look first at their autocratic political traditions, the results of World War I, and the devastation of the Great Depression.

Japan is the longest continuous monarchy in the world, and is in part based on its Shinto religion. According to Japanese tradition, emperors were more like deities. By the time Harry had graduated, the emperor had become "sacred and inviolable." Although sovereignty rested with him, his main role was to ratify and give the imperial stamp of approval to decisions made by the nationalistic militarists clamoring for dictatorship and the creation of a Japanese sphere of influence, much like what they saw belonging to colonial Western powers including the United States. As General Sadao Araki stated, "It is Japan's mission to be supreme in Asia, the South Seas and eventually the four corners of the world."[17]

After World War I, the British, French, American, Russian, and even the Dutch could have sung the version of the old spiritual "We've Got the Whole World in Our Hands." They had spheres of influence everywhere in Asia, especially where the Japanese felt they were best suited to rule. The Japanese only had control of Korea and small parts of China.

The United States saw as its goal to stop what they saw as "rising Japanese militarism." Not surprisingly, this pissed off the Japanese to no end. They felt as if they were second class to British and American imperialists, even in their own backyard. Add to these indignities the United States passing the Japanese Exclusion Act of 1924, a "ban" that prohibited Japanese immigration into the United States. The Japanese saw these "racist" actions as reasons to move the Japanese toward xenophobic and Asia-centric positions. Ninety plus years later and we still haven't learned.

The ramifications of the Great Depression provoked spiraling prices, unemployment, and falling exports, which resulted in social unrest. By May 1932, admirals ruled Japan. The idea of the "Greater East Asian Co-Prosperity Sphere" emerged. This led to Pearl Harbor.

Did the men and women of Harry's age understand what was brewing in Asia? Did they care? Most on the east coast, being of European descent, merely skimmed the articles about Asia. Some did read and were becoming increasingly troubled.

The Japanese had already invaded China, The *New York Times* reported that, "Within six months we shall be applying the sanctions of Article XVI of the [League of Nations] covenant against Japan, one of Europe's most experienced and farsighted Foreign Ministers predicted privately the other day."[18] This threat did nothing but to have the Japanese walk out.

In December 1934, Japanese Ambassador Hirosi Saito, in a very Machiavellian statement said, "that Japan's main idea is to establish law and order, peace, and prosperity. To forward that idea we shall do what we consider appropriate."[19]

By 1937 things got worse. Backward and broken, China had no chance against Japan's modern army. One of the worst military holocausts in history occurred in Nanking where Japanese troops slaughtered an estimated 300,000 civilians and raped 80,000 women. Torture, rape, and disfigurement were common. Think of the casualties in Syria but over 6 weeks, not 6 years.

How much of this did Harry and his cohort know or care about? Could all this have gone unnoticed by politically astute college students? I doubt it. All of this had taken place by the end of 1937, when Harry was right out of college. The men and women of City College knew. They had to. They may have ignored it, but they knew. Maybe it was too far away and they knew few Chinese here in New York except when they ordered "combination plate #1" in Chinatown.

Italy was another story. Brooklyn and New York City had a huge Italian population. Also, a former monarchy, Italy entered World War I on the side of the Allies as the result of the Treaty of London in 1915. Unfortunately, the same Treaty of Versailles that disrespected the Japanese did so as well to the Italians. It forced Italy to accept only two small areas from Austria. The coveted Adriatic coast was made part of a new country to be called Yugoslavia.

So, you can fully understand why Italy became the second pissed off "winner" of The Great War. That anger fueled the rise of "Il Duce," Benito Mussolini, who later cited the treaty for Italy's 1939 alliance with Nazi Germany. The Fascists supported nationalist sentiments, hoping to raise Italy to levels of its great Roman past.

"Make Italy Great Again" became his theme. Mussolini and his Fascists replaced the Italian monarchy during the early 1920s as a result of the treaty and its aftermath.

Mussolini rose to power by using his private army of "Black Shirts" to intimidate and his oratory style to persuade. Staccato and repetitive, he rarely failed to impose his mood. He was highly theatrical. His opinions were contradictory. His facts were often wrong, and his attacks were frequently malicious and misdirected; but his words were so dramatic, his metaphors so apt and striking, his vigorous, repetitive gestures so extraordinarily effective, that he easily won people over. Perhaps he would have made a great, a really great, winning presidential candidate. He provided Italians with his own version of "fake news."

(*Author's note:* Any references to a certain orange haired presidential candidate and election winner in 2016 are "merely a coincidence".)

Mahatma Gandhi, yes that Mahatma Gandhi, called Mussolini "one of the great statesmen of our time." In the mid-1920s, Winston Churchill met Mussolini and said, "If I had been Italian, I am sure I would have been with you from the beginning."[20] Scary isn't it?

How did he gain that critical acclaim? Much of Europe had a post–World War I depression that closely compared with the "great" one 10 years later. Under Il Duce, "Between 1921 and 1925, the Italian economy grew more than 20 percent. Unemployment fell 77 percent."[21] Some say FDR modeled some New Deal programs after his. At least he was successful.

Then Il Duce went in search of a sphere of influence. In 1935 he invaded Ethiopia and created his version of a "new Roman Empire." It took his modern army of approximately 800,000 seven months to crush the Ethiopian army of around 500,000 men, some of whom were armed with nothing more than spears and bows.

But I digress. I assume that these knowledge-hungry collegians read this too, especially those of Italian descent. Some may have been shocked. Others were more likely filled with pride about their parental homeland.

Finally, there is Germany. It is no surprise that many Americans followed what went on in Germany during the 1920s and 1930s far more than in Italy or Japan. It is impossible to believe Harry and his fellow students ignored what occurred there. The growth of the Nazi party in Germany and Adolf Hitler's totalitarian dictatorship had the most effect on American kids who, like Harry, were Americans of Austrian, German, or Jewish descent. It had to spread fear especially among those of Jewish descent. Eighty years later dare we ask the same question of the United States?

How much did these American college graduates know about Adolf Hitler? Did they know of his failed "Beer Hall Putsch" (revolt) in 1923? Did they read Hitler's revealing book, *Mein Kampf*, published in 1925 with its clearly laid out plans for a Third Reich? Did they know the book publicly stated his philosophies of Lebenstraum and The Big Lie and how to deal with the Jewish question for all to see when it was translated into English during their senior year in college? What did they and their fellow Americans know and believe about him and the Nazi Party? Did they know what the National Socialist Party stood for? Hitler tells us straight out.

> *The Parties of class warfare may be sure that as long as the Almighty lets me live my determination to destroy them will be unconquerable.... We want a break with what a rotten brand of democracy has produced and realize that all that is great can be created only by the strength of an individual personality and that all that is to be preserved must be entrusted again to ability and individual personality, while the parliamentary-democratic system must be fought.*[22]

Was the system "rigged" too? Was he proposing to "clean up the swamp?"

How did they react? This was three weeks before FDR's "The only thing we have to fear is fear itself" speech. Americans had just elected their own strong personality to save them from the depths of the Depression. Was this "nutty" Hitler character just a German version, or did they see him as a real threat? Did they even pay attention?

On September 3 of that year the *New York Times* quoted him again.

> *We have declared a hundred times that we do not wish war with the rest of the world, nor do we want to incorporate anything that is alien to us. But if treaties [referring to the Versailles Treaty] are to be sacred then they shall be sacred not only for us but for our opponents as well.*[23]

Was that a veiled threat just eight months after taking office?

By the time Harry graduated college Hitler had already violated the Treaty of Versailles,

withdrew from the League of Nations, began rapid rearmament, signed a nonaggression pact with Poland, reacquired the Saar territory [from France] through a plebiscite, militarily assisted the supporters of Francisco Franco in the Spanish Civil War, and remilitarized the Rhineland.[24]

Fooling around he wasn't. The dark side of the Force was indeed growing in power.

If this wasn't troubling to these college-educated, well-read Jewish New Yorkers, what was going on within Germany had to be downright frightening, but by the time Harry and his college colleagues graduated in the spring of 1937 Hitler's economic policies were embraced worldwide. Regarding domestic affairs, some might say he sounded a bit Rooseveltian. Or Trumpian? The Times reported Hitler's plans as follows.

The National Government, with iron will and tenacious perseverance, will realize the following plan: within four years the German farmer will be relieved from impoverishment; within four years unemployment must be definitely overcome. Concurrently, conditions will be established for prosperity in the other branches of industry.[25]

Just as FDR's massive programs to rebuild the US economy made great strides, so did Hitler's.

By 1934, just a year after Hitler's election, unemployment had been halved, to 3 million. From March 1933 March 1934. Here, agricultural unemployment dramatically fell from 238,000 to 60,000, and construction unemployment fell from 493,000 to 107,000. Though the figures may be filtered through the propaganda network of the Reich, a radical drop in unemployment did occur. Potentially, unemployment dropped from 6 million in 1933, to 302,000 in 1939.[26]

What made Germany even more successful than the United States in the employment picture was that in Germany the new army and Nazi bureaucracy now became the nation's largest employers.

#JEWISHLIVESMATTER

Hitler had kept his promises. How many of those Brooklyn Nazi sympathizers and members of a growing American Nazi Party felt proud of the way Germany rebounded from the humiliating loss of World War I, the Versailles Treaty, and the Great Depression under its new and powerful leader who came up from the rank and file of workers and soldiers? One can also imagine how they strongly agreed with his anti-Semitic view and his fight against "the Jewish Bolshevistic terror." One only has to look at the trail of tears he produced in Germany.

> *Hitler's economic policies cannot be divorced from his great policies of virulent anti-Semitism, racism and genocide ... Analyzing his actions through any other lens severely misses the point.*[27]

This was reported as early as June 12, 1933, when Abraham Herman, president of the Hebrew Immigration Aid Society told an audience of 960 about the three recourses for German Jews, "These are economic extinction, emigration, or suicide."

"Jews throughout America were asked to finance the emigration of their brethren to refugees in other lands." Isador Apfel, Grand Master of B'rith Abraham went further. "The very existence of Jews in Germany is threatened by wild and barbaric hatred." It was also reported that day that US Senators Robinson, Wagner, Hatfield, and Walsh had "denounced Nazi anti-Semitism."[28] The quote is of Herman stated above.

Even if one only skimmed the *New York Times,* this June 1933 headline would have made you think:

HITLERISM LIKENED TO LYNCH LAW HERE
Reich Seen in Revolution[29]

Harry's family had personal information about what was going on in Berlin. Someone in the family, probably Harry's mom, received this letter from a relative (although spelled differently) still in Berlin dated September 17, 1933.

The most telling line in the letter (written in a combination of Yiddish and German) tells the American Greissmans that:

I am trying to sell everything and travel to Palestine. F.S. has little hope.

Why are they trying to sell everything? April 1, 1933, the Nazis carried out the first nationwide, planned action against them: a boycott of Jewish businesses. Nazi spokesmen claimed the boycott was an act of revenge against both German Jews and foreigners who had criticized the Nazi regime. On the day of the boycott, Storm Troopers stood menacingly in front of Jewish-owned shops. The six-pointed "Star of David " was painted in yellow and black across thousands of doors and windows.

The Berlin Greissmans were trying to sell everything and go to Palestine for good reason. They saw the handwriting on the wall. As far as we know, they did not make it to Palestine.

September 1935 marked a new low in European history, the establishment of the so-called Nuremberg Laws. As early as September 3, 1935, the *New York Times* reported on the speech of Joseph Goebbels, Reich Minister of Propaganda, on the "racial question."

In every district, every city and every village, they will receive this viewpoint and almost all will accept it. And the burden of the talks was a defense and justification of the Nazi racial policy with regard to the Jews, a rousing invitation to the rest of the world to imitate it and a confident prediction that most of the world will do so.

Ironically, at the end of World War II, in his capacity of military translator in interrogations of German prisoners and refugees, Harry collected the actual pamphlets used in this endeavor. Goebbels was also quoted as saying:

We used the weapons and rules of democracy but only to bring it to a fall and to eliminate it from German life. National Socialism is consciously on the defensive against the excesses of liberalism. But you cannot understand this unless you pay special attention to the Jewish question. Foreign countries have criticized us unjustly. We have been trying to solve the Jewish question practically. It was but one question of many and it is international Jewry's fault that is has become almost exclusively the problem of world discussion.

Think that is harsh? He continues:

Yet at the beginning of our regime we were reserved in our treatment of the Jews. That more stringent measures were adopted is due exclusively to world Jewry. If this meant material harm to the Jews who remained in Germany, let them thank their own people abroad for it. Not a hair of a Jew was rumpled without reason.

What more stringent measures? To what is he referring? We didn't have to wait long.

Starting on September 15, 1935, Germany passed a series of laws and regulations commonly called "The Nuremberg Laws." Regardless of how any individual identified his or her self, the law now defined anyone with three or four Jewish grandparents as a Jew. As all others living within German borders, Jews had to carry "papers," but theirs had a big "J" stamped on them.

Why was it now necessary to easily identify Jews? The first law revoked their citizenship and all rights reserved to citizens. Therefore, they lost all legal and civil rights to fight against any now legal persecution by the government as well as the loss of the right to sue in civil court any German who violated their person or personal property. All Jews were now fair game.

Over the next months and years (with a brief respite before and during the Berlin Olympic Games for PR reasons) Jews had their property and businesses registered and then "Aryanized." Jewish workers and managers were dismissed, and non-Jewish "pure" Aryan Germans seized Jewish properties, including homes, for pennies on the Mark. Jewish doctors and lawyers could no longer practice their trades. Jewish teachers and professors would no longer be able to work in German schools. Jewish journalist? Stock broker? Sorry! You are out of work as well.

One month later a new law was passed entitled, the "Law for the Protection of the Hereditary Health of the German People." This required all prospective marriage partners to obtain a certificate of fitness to marry. Fitness meant no one suffering from what they called "hereditary illnesses" and contagious diseases, and obviously those trying to avoid the first law. Finally, another month later brought a supplemental decree to extend those prohibitions to people who could produce "racially suspect" offspring, now including Roma (Gypsies) and Blacks.

On September 16 the *New York Times* provided Hitler's text as he addressed the Reichstag. On November 16 it reported:

REICH PUTS LAWS ON JEWS IN FORCE:
Decrees Execute Nuremberg Acts Banning Citizenship
and Intermarriage[30]

Reactions here varied.

Hitler wanted to promote German greatness and his ideals/laws of racial purity through the 1936 Olympic games to be held in Berlin. But when faced with the possible boycott of several nations, including the United States, he allowed the teams of other nations to include Jews. Most notably, many Jewish athletes from other nations were sidelined.

The worst offender was the United States. Many Americans are quite proud of Jesse Owens's winning four gold medals, but how many know that one of them was only because two Jewish athletes, Sam Stoller and Marty Glickman, were told they would not be running in the 4 × 100 relay. During the entire history of US participation in the Olympic games, Glickman and Stoller were the only two members of the US Olympic team who did not compete after arriving at the site of the games.

The *New York Times*, on August 8, 1936, reported that track and field coach Lawson Robertson was replacing Stoller and Glickman, but not one word was used to indicate that anti-Semitism was the cause. In fact, Jesse Owens's track coach, Larry Snyder, had predicted that Stoller and Glickman would join Owens on that team and handily win.[31]

In the late 1980s I had the honor of meeting Marty Glickman, who had become a world famous sports broadcaster. A fellow social studies teacher and I created a project for our high school senior classes putting Avery Brundage, the head of the 1936 Olympic committee, on trial. Glickman, who lived close by, was our chief witness against Brundage. His words tell the story best. This is the transcript of him speaking about his experiences from the United States Holocaust Museum.

> *I was always aware of the fact that I am a Jew, never unaware of it, under virtually all circumstances. Even in the high school competitions, and certainly at college and for the Olympic team, I wanted to show that a Jew could do just as well as any other individual no matter what his race, creed, or color, and perhaps even better.*
>
> *The Olympic stadium itself is a very impressive place. It was particularly impressive then, filled with 120,000 people. When Hitler walked into the stadium,*

stands would rise, and you'd hear it in unison, "Sieg Heil, Sieg Heil," all together, this huge sound reverberating through the stadium.

Everyone seemed to be in uniform. As for banners and flags, they were all over the place, dominated by the swastika. The swastika was all over. On virtually every other banner we saw, there was a swastika. But this was 1936; this was before we really got to know what the swastika truly meant.

There was anti-Semitism in Germany. I knew that. And there was anti-Semitism in America. In New York City, I was also aware of the fact that there were certain places I was not welcome. You went into a hotel, for example, and you'd see a small sign where you registered which read "Restricted clientele," which meant, in effect, no Jews or Blacks allowed.

The event I was supposed to run, the 400-meter relay, was one of the last events in the track and field program. The morning of the day we were supposed to run in the trial heats, we were called into a meeting, the seven sprinters were, along with Dean Cromwell, the assistant track coach, and Lawson Robertson, the head track coach. Robertson announced to the seven of us that he had heard very strong rumors that the Germans were saving their best sprinters, hiding them, to upset the American team in the 400-meter relay. Consequently, Sam Stoller and I were to be replaced by Jesse Owens and Ralph Metcalfe.

We were shocked. Sam was completely stunned. He didn't say a word in the meeting. I was a brash 18-year-old kid and I said, "Coach, you can't hide world-class sprinters." At which point, Jesse spoke up and said "Coach, I've won my 3 gold medals [the 100, the 200, and the long jump]. I'm tired. I've had it. Let Marty and Sam run, they deserve it," said Jesse. And Cromwell pointed his finger at him and said, "You'll do as you're told." And in those days, black athletes did as they were told, and Jesse was quiet after that.

Watching the final the following day, I see Metcalfe passing runners down the backstretch, he ran the second leg, and [I thought] "that should be me out there. That should be me. That's me out there." I as an 18-year-old, just out of my fresh-man year, I vowed that come 1940 I'd win it all. I'd win the 100, the 200; I'd run on the relay. I was going to be 22 in 1940. I was a good athlete, I knew that, and 4 years hence I was going to be out there again. Of course, 1940 never came. There was a war on. 1944 never came.[32]

Glickman, only two years younger than Harry, lived in Brooklyn where he was a big track star at James Madison High School. Harry also was a Jewish athlete from New York. He had to have known about Glickman. He had to have known what happened to Glickman and Stoller.

How did the folks at City College's School of Business and Civic Administration's *Ticker* react? After all, a majority of the students there were of Jewish descent. The *Ticker*, of which Harry was editor in chief, positioned itself as early as March 11, 1934, when it said,

Herr Hitler is feverishly engaged in the armament of Germany, an activity which has thrown France and England into panic armament competition. The God of War has unsheathed his sword and is taking a few practice swings. Another conflagration will inevitably consume the entire world and result in the complete destruction of civilization, as we know it. No nation can remain aloof.

Harry had to have written, "The God of War has unsheathed his sword and is taking a few practice swings."

One student, Israel Cohen, wrote a letter to the editors pleading for the paper to devote more space to the pressing militaristic issues and Fascism the world was facing from Germany, Italy, and Japan. Yet nowhere in his letter does he refer specifically to the Nuremberg laws.[33]

On March 25, 1935, the *Ticker's* lead editorial titled "War and the Student" indicated they were very aware of the threat of war. "War is more imminent today than at any time since the World War. As intelligent students it is imperative that we register our protest against these conditions." Some 600 students attended a symposium on the subject.

So, it seems that if Harry's classmates were representative of college kids in the mid-1930s. It is quite clear that even as underclassmen Harry and his classmates were well aware of what the future may hold in store for them. We seem to forget that student demonstrations predate the Civil Rights and antiwar protests of the 1960s and 1970s. As much pain and suffering may have been occurring in other places of the world, they, like we, became more focused on joining antiwar movements, perhaps because war was as dangerous to them as well as it was to us. War means the possibility of losing your life or the lives of loved ones. They were about to embark on the journey that would be the rest of their lives. The next four years would determine who lived, who died, who laughed, and who cried.

#OPTOUTOFWAR

By the time the 1940 census was taken, the world was already at war. Young men Harry's age had already started to enlist. Harry's older brother, Abraham, had already served the military from April 24, 1924, through April 28, 1928, as a pharmacists mate, seaman 2nd class. He served on the USS *Camden* and USS *Lark* before being based at the submarine base in New London, Connecticut. According to his discharge papers, he was "furnished travel allowance" back to Brooklyn "at the rate of 5 cents per mile." The monthly rate of pay when he was discharged? $79.20!

Abraham would reenlist in the Coast Guard in Washington, DC, in September 7, 1942. He worked for the United States Information Agency (known as the United States Information Service prior to 1953) where he would return and work until his death in January 1968.

That is Abe right in the front in this undated picture.

Starting in the mid-1930s the United States passed a series of neutrality acts that prohibited the sale of arms, munitions, implements of war, and making any loans to any belligerent nation. The Neutrality Act of 1937 added that US citizens were forbidden from traveling on belligerent ships, and American merchant ships were prevented from transporting arms to belligerents even if those arms were produced outside of the United States. The act gave the president the authority to bar all belligerent ships from US waters, and to extend the export embargo to any additional articles or materials.

The antiwar sentiment in the United States had had no effect on the events in Europe and Asia. In 1936, while Harry was still in college, the Germans had already moved troops into the demilitarized zone of the Rhineland between Germany and its western neighbors. In March 1938 Hitler annexed Austria in what he called "Anschluss." Hitler then laid claim to the area of Czechoslovakia bordering Germany called the Sudetenland. On September 30 he signed the infamous Munich Agreement, where the major European powers allowed him to take the Sudetenland with a promise of "no more." British PM Neville Chamberlain's quote that this agreement would bring "peace in our time" showed the West's weakness.

In March, the rest of Czechoslovakia became German. On Friday, September 1, 1939, Harry read this. He and others knew their time was coming.

http://www.nytimes.com/learning/general/onthisday/big/0901.html

After the Germans invaded Poland in September 1939 the world chose sides like in a Brooklyn stickball game. Japan, remember Japan, was still hard at work at creating its so-called Co-Prosperity Sphere. The Japanese, now allies of Germany and Italy and seeing the opportunity to grab "Allied" colonial possessions, went on the warpath against their mutual enemies England and France. They invaded French Indochina. They secretly plotted to gain control of British colonies, and especially desired those territories jointly claimed by the USSR, or controlled by their biggest threat in the Pacific, the United States.

Citizens of the United States watched from across the Atlantic and Pacific. Worried that the United States would be swept up into the hell of war, yet also wanting to be prepared for it, we tried to work both ends against the middle. On September 5, the United States declared neutrality.

Two months after the invasion of Poland, FDR was able stay out of the war yet help obvious allies through the Lend Lease Act passed in December 1940. This was most notable when the United States gave the British fifty old destroyers in exchange for 99-year leases of bases in Newfoundland and the Caribbean. Through it,

> *The United States would provide Great Britain with the supplies it needed to fight Germany, but would not insist upon being paid immediately. Instead, the United States would "lend" the supplies to the British, deferring payment. When payment eventually did take place, the emphasis would not be on payment in dollars.*[34]

Harry and his ordinary twentysomething buddies had to have seen what was coming, but they tried to live life as normally as they could. In 1940, as most single young men of that time, he was still living in Brooklyn with his parents. However, in May 1940, he applied for his Social Security card using the name Harry Grant Greissman. This is the only record of the use of Grant as a middle name. Was it for fear of being too "Jewish"?

Louis's daughter Susan remembers,

> *My father told me that he used the name "Grant" in advertising because it wasn't so Jewish. I actually used it as a middle name for my son, Damon Grant Beaudry, side stepping naming him after a living person.*

The 1940 census has Harry listed as a sporting goods salesman having made $1,000 in 1939. Who knew? Today, we are all positive it was to allow him to immerse himself in tennis paraphernalia. It must have been disappointing for Harry and his family that he was selling sporting goods after four accolade-filled years at college. However, the depression still lingered and they were happy that everyone in the family had a job that brought money into the household.

Abe, Solomon, Harry, and Louis were all potential draftees if the United States joined the war. Only oldest brother Jake was exempt. Their generation suffered from a duality of patriotism and fear. The boys were no exception.

From the start of the war, soon to be called World War II, things looked very bad for those nations most friendly to the United States. By the end of September Germany conquered Poland. The month before Russia and Germany signed an agreement that publicly stated Germany would exchange manufactured goods for Soviet raw materials and included a ten-year long non-aggression pact, promising not to attack each other during that time period. Secretly, however, it also provided for the partition of Poland and the rest of Eastern Europe into Germany and Soviet spheres of interests. By October the two "allies" divided Poland.

By the end of spring 1940 the Soviets conquered Finland while Germany overtook Denmark, Norway, and the Netherlands. In May, Germany invaded France. French and British soldiers suffered a famously embarrassing retreat across the English Channel from Dunkirk, France. The Germans entered Paris, the "city of light" in mid-June and forced France to surrender on June 22. German submarines began to attack ships travelling in the Atlantic Ocean. German planes had already started air raids on England. Germans registered Jews in Amsterdam.

All of this appeared in every daily newspaper and on the news reels that appeared before every film in movie theaters all over the country. Sixty thousand National Guardsmen were activated. Finally, a little after a year following the invasion of Poland, the US Congress established the first peacetime draft in US history. All men ages 21–35 had to register with local draft boards. One month later 16 million men registered. The first draftees were selected in December 1940, a year before the attack on Pearl Harbor. Harry was 24.

Clearly the handwriting was on the wall.

Things kept looking bad. Roosevelt announced that the United States must become an "arsenal of democracy." There were rumors of a planned Japanese attack on military outposts like Pearl Harbor. The tension those young men and their families felt became palpable. I can understand that. Many of my generation felt that as the Vietnam War grew. Even though the draft still existed, many men like me had deferments that had been ended in 1969. Most of us faced the trauma of whether or not we would be called to war. In 1940, the difference was that war seemed everywhere. Similarly though, before the attack on Pearl Harbor, there was a big antiwar movement. Worry and fear were two things in common.

The draft made military service compulsory for Harry, but others in the family faced more dire circumstances. Jacob Greissman received an airmail letter sent on December 12, 1940, from Anna (Harry's mom's half-sister) and Maurice Aronsfrau from 198 Goldhurst Terrace, London, N.W. 6 (near the Beatles' famous Abbey Road Studios). The letter had already been opened and read by "Examiner 6229."

The letter was in thanks for affidavits sent to them in an attempt to get a non-quota visa to help her brother and sister-in-law. Although the American Consul admired them, she explains, "What a pity, they cannot help." "Nothing can help. Only a wife or husband can petition for a non-quota visa." She went on to say that she was advised that her brother and sister-in-law would have to wait about two years for their Polish quota visa. That was extremely problematic given the events, even though the couple was in Portugal, not Poland. The couple's children, born in Belgium, were to leave to the United States shortly because the Belgian quota was open. Two US immigration laws had been passed in the 1920s limiting immigrants from various countries based on nationality. Strict quotas were kept. They were overturned in 1965. These laws precede Trump's plan to prohibit Muslims. It seems to be what we do.

Anna and Maurice, being American and British, were free to return to the United States when they wanted, but even that was complicated by all the "neutrality acts." Anna, as an American could come on a US ship, but Maurice had to take a British boat. He refused to travel without her. They would have to wait for an American steamer.

In February 1941 Jacob received a letter mysteriously postmarked in Staten Island but written in Lisbon by Sophie Kanerek Aronsfrau, Maurice's sister, "an unknown cousin." This is her story.

> *We left Antwerp at the beginning of the war and after a few miserable months wandering all over France, we succeeded at last to reach Lisbon. Like most people, our biggest wish is to come to America but to get there we need a lot of papers. Although my husband has a bank account in New York and is very well known in business, the American Consul advises us to obtain these necessary papers from American relatives.... We are five and need a financial affidavit with the income taxes as proof, a political, and a moral affidavit as proof.*

She then goes on to list the five names along with their birthdates. She and her husband, Meyer Kanerek are 62 and 60. Their children (the oldest appears to be a son-in-law) are 49, 39, and 28. In March 1941 Jacob received a telegram stating they had not yet received the affidavits. According to Geni.com, they made it. Meyer, a diamond importer, died April 1966 in New York, NY, USA. Sophie wasn't as lucky. Although she did get to the United States, she died in New York only a year after she wrote the letter, in April 1942.[35]

And Harry? What about Harry? This is a story about Harry. Where is he? It seems somehow he ended up in Hammond, Indiana, a suburb of Chicago. In a letter postmarked January 31, 1941, to his brother Jack (Jacob), Harry starts off by describing what would be known by many as a very Harry thing to do. He apologizes for the lateness of this particular letter because he "came across a letter addressed to you about *2 weeks ago*, that I had forgotten to mail."

Why? He left it in a jacket pocket. We can place the time as late 1940 to early 1941 as the biopic, Knute Rockne, was released on October 4, 1940, and there is no mention of the draft.

> *Dear Jack,*
>
> *Everything about this piece will be somebody else's but the words. The type-writer belongs to one of the college boys in my rooming house, the stationary to the son of one of Canton, O's magnates, and the light belongs to the house....*
>
> *Had my first bit of dissipation last night since coming here. Went to Chicago to see a friend of a friend and she was very fine.*

Since *dissipation* is defined as "a descent into drunkenness and sexual dissipation," one can only imagine Harry's use of the word *fine.*

Showed me the town in real style, especially the magnificent Wrigley Building, with its incredible lighting effects. Also saw "Knute Rockne" in one of Chi's more palatial movie houses. Got home at 1:30 AM, which is by a long shot the latest I've been up since being here.

Well, Sir, things are beginning to take more definite shape now.... To be honest about it, I was a little bit leery about how long it would take for me to get back into the swing of newspaper ad production. I didn't let it scare me, though, and I think I've come along okay ... and in a couple of weeks the acid test will come.

About our prospects out here, I wish I could believe salesmen. The sales manager, along with the advertising manager of Emerson Radio was up to the office the other day and spent half a day with us. They were absolutely raving about our set-up, and have allocated us a $500 advtsg budget for the X-Mas period alone.... And speaking of radios, sir, and getting ahead of myself a bit—I'm picking one out with fine tone and shipping it to you.

He inquires about his brother Sol's new venture and Abe's civil service exam and exclaims, "Maybe us G-men will amount to a roll of pins after all." A what? I can't find that expression anywhere.

This week I am going into my first two-color work with newspapers and have my fingers crossed. I've never tackled anything in color before, but one of the better Evanston gazettes has promised to open a special color supplement for me, and I'm going to try it with my little artistic flair. Sometimes I wish I had good old Lou out here—what a production job he could do with the kind of money I have to play with. [Lou is another one of his older brothers....]

He sends regards to other family members and the Kaisers (friends, not German emperors) and a slew of others before he thanks Jack for giving him a "blanket source" at Franklin Textiles that "we" used to strike a deal. For whom did Harry work? Was it Hammond Jewelers, a diamond seller? Was it a department store that sold everything from blankets to radios? Was it an ad agency? We never find out who "we" and "us" are. Then he signs off in German, "auffwidersehen." Was Harry being bilingual or is this an attempt at sarcasm?

Jew's in the
Army Now

Fort Bragg is located just outside of Fayetteville, North Carolina. Our young soldiers adjusted to a new life.

On Saturday, May 3, 1941, Harry writes Jack, his wife Rose, and daughters Edie and Judie. As all good draftees, he thanked them for goodies sent through another typical Harryism,

> *In more than a pun, they hit the spot—in fact my entire platoon. In matters of food and idyllic sort of communism prevails here—when one of the boys gets a package, it's passed around for the edification of all. We're supposed to be in the most pictur-esque fort in this country—& on days like this, we all agree. We did go through a dust and thunder storm in which our barracks walls and windows trembled like straws in the wind—we all got more than a mouthful of sand out of it, but work went on as usual.*

At first Harry was assigned to the Battery Commander's office, as he calls it "a pleasant place to be—but I get a lot of drilling in anyway." He describes the office being run much like a business. He started off doing more typing but gradually "was left more on my own initiative scheduling the week's drills and details" being "excused from the more sordid 'fatigue' drills like kitchen police and latrine patrol (each of which I was given at Fort Dix for 'breaches' of discipline)."

He goes on.

> *None of us know where we go from here but if I can keep my nose clean, a good record here will help me get my transfer to the kind of work I prefer.*

A guy is likely to end up anywhere.

P.S. My left arm is holding up okay although it failed me completely on the rifle range—couldn't steady the gun no how.

That must have explained the office duty. A week later he writes again, after hearing back from Jack and the clan. Apparently he started, "building up a diary of incidents and personalities I won't quickly forget….Strangely enough my best pal out here is that proverbial terror of all ages, the top Kick (1st Sergeant) … real southern stock, graceful as a peacock in his carriage and military manners and at age 38, a veteran of 21 years' service in the army."

(http://www.craveonline.com/site/198151-the-myth-of-macho-full-metal-jacket)

Think of the sergeant from the movie *Full Metal Jacket*. How did this New York Jewish intellectual become the righthand man of what many would probably call a typical Southern cracker? His buddy, "the top Kick," set it up so he was "the only guy who didn't have to stand Reveille or Retreat (morning and evening assemblies)." Harry's service stint so far seems like a sitcom, with the Southern Reb and the NY Jew in lead roles.

Before I came along, he tells me, he practically ran our Battery by himself- now he has included me as part of the works.

Harry would now "handle the Commanding Officer's correspondence, dole out punishment for petty offenses like A.W.O.L. and try to act like some sort of liaison between the officers and troops in matters of mess, discipline, and special orders."

In this 1941 pic of the Fort Bragg crew we see examples of Harry's "punnish" behavior. *"Follies of the Fort ... or Nothing to Bragg about!"*

Next Year: East Lynne [refers to a 1931 movie portraying a group of British soldiers during World War 1 stage a comic performance of the play East Lynne to entertain their comrades.] By Hi-Ho-Hee-To. Extra added Distraction: Japsy Rose Tee. [His "actors" are, left to right,] "Sam the Pastor, Phil, the fighting fool ... our @#$% cook, Van, always on the Move, Harry in the dress uniform, Jack, Doughboy Model '41, and Swivel Stack Charlie, our cook by hook.

He finishes the letter by talking about an inter-platoon baseball game his team won and as a result won free beer. He ponders heading out for Pinehurst with his tennis racquet and stirring up some "extracurricular excitement that way."

Harry's letters home often included discussions about siblings. What happened to his brother Saul? A letter by Harry in June expresses:

> *shock at the finality of Saul's case—we get no papers to speak of here—and so your news about Saul's reentry into the advertising indicated that the wolves had indeed sunk their claws into another white man.... I doubt Saul was serious enough enmeshed in politics outside of college to merit any judgment in that witch hunt, but these, it seems, are times when a whisper of suspicion rings louder than the loudest thundering of truth—when any of us are subject by trial by nightmare or slightest provocation.... and that in some certain Hell, the people behind that little witch hunt, the Rapps? And Cudares? And the others behind the scenes find their own reward.*

After talking about his two beautiful nieces Edie and Judie, Harry went back to talking about his work at the fort and his future.

> *About this talk of going to Officer's training school—That is out completely. I don't want an army career and if I could get out in a year with no glory or no stripes of any kind, I'll exit smiling and happier. I have received basic officer's training in calculating firing data for the big cannon and while I did quite well with that, am not pushing the issue—in fact I already told my C.O. my precise sentiments so there is no danger of my being pushed into unwelcome advancement. Things change overnight in the army, but at present, my status is this: if our group does not go up north on our next move, I will remain here as N.C.O. charge of Battery. It will be a pleasant job indefinitely if we go to war by mid-summer—a prospect that becomes more and more imminent....*

Somehow he was made "#1 on the Fayetteville County Tennis Club" team and was playing against Greensboro the following week.

> *There may be pictures and a story in the town daily.... Having a grand time with my tennis friends in town—meeting some fine, simple people ... and my weekends really profit from the racket.*

How had this little Jewish kid from Brooklyn played tennis for a southern tennis team where notorious bias and anti-Semitism reigned supreme? Clubs in New York wouldn't let Jews play.

And what did he mean by that play on words "and my weekends really profit from the racket." Was he making money from the use of his racquet racket?

By July, Harry had been promoted to the rank of corporal. In September 1941, Harry, still at Fort Bragg, wrote this.

> *The news on the Washington front doesn't look or sound so good, does it? What are the odds on war by fall? It's pretty hard to look at the sunny side of things when there's so little sun to see, but I guess there have been drearier times than these and the world has suffered thru its troubles to the year 1941 A.D.*
>
> *Life here in the army continues to be a campus of cannons instead of canons. [Lord, what a phrase!] I was allowed to join the Officers Golf Club and play on their fine links whenever opportunity provides for the munificent fee of $.75 a month.*

One of Harry's new trainees was an Iowan golf champ who caddied for him and helped him cut his scores down to the low nineties.

> *I play golf twice a week and tennis 3 times a week.... Did I tell you that I passed my government driver's test after a week's practice and now have a command car*

at my disposal for use in the fort? Sure is a satisfying thrill to pick up driving that quickly and these days these gov't cars are more intricate than civilians, with their 8 speeds forward and 2 speeds in reverse. Takes a mighty tough obstacle to stop one of these cars.

Harry's army life was a hell of a lot different than most. Tennis? Golf? Did the man work? They let Harry drive his own car? We knew him as the world's worst driver. The evidence: a driver's license, a pass car, and an ID. The license allows him to "operate any motor vehicle in the army, except motorcycles." Does that include a tank? The back of his pass card has a list of 15 dates from 5/11/41 to 8/17/41. I imagine they were a list of days he went off "campus." Yet at this time neither Harry nor his buddies knew exactly what their fates would be.

DAYS OF INFAMY

M en in the military "knew" they would eventually go off to war against Germany. All the news pointed to it. Then Pearl Harbor, the US Naval base in Hawaii was attacked on the morning of December 7, 1941. On December 8, 1941, FDR described December 7, 1941, as "a date which will live in infamy" in his speech asking Congress to declare war on Japan. All Americans huddled around their radios.

The United States of America was suddenly and deliberately attacked by naval and air forces of the Empire of Japan. The United States was at peace with that nation and, at the solicitation of Japan, was still in conversation with its government and its emperor looking toward the maintenance of peace in the Pacific. Indeed, one hour after Japanese air squadrons had commenced bombing in the American island of Oahu, the Japanese ambassador to the United States and his colleague delivered to our Secretary of State a formal reply to a recent American message. And while this reply stated that it seemed useless to continue the existing diplomatic negotiations, it contained no threat or hint of war or of armed attack.

The attack yesterday on the Hawaiian islands has caused severe damage to American naval and military forces. I regret to tell you that very many American lives have been lost. In addition, American ships have been reported torpedoed on the high seas between San Francisco and Honolulu.

Yesterday, the Japanese government also launched an attack against Malaya.

Last night, Japanese forces attacked Hong Kong.
Last night, Japanese forces attacked Guam.
Last night, Japanese forces attacked the Philippine Islands.
Last night, the Japanese attacked Wake Island.
And this morning, the Japanese attacked Midway Island.[36]

The news shocked the nation. In May and June 1942 Harry wrote two significantly shorter letters to Jack and his family. Each refers to a separate furlough. There is nothing much about work, except that it keeps him on the run and that there is a "whistle calling me back to duty." He adds in the May letter that "if I don't write as much as I'd like it is only because there is so much to be done here, and so little time to do it." The June letter only mentions a short statement he had written once before,

War picture doesn't look so good, does it?

No, it didn't. By July 1942, Nazi Germany, Fascist Italy, and Imperial Japan formally aligned as the Axis Powers. The Germans sent troops into North Africa. Nazi Germany and its Axis partners invaded the Soviet Union, overran the Baltic States, lay siege to Leningrad as they captured Kiev by September, and attacked Moscow by October. And that was just in Europe.

From Pearl Harbor through the July day when Harry wrote his next letter, the news in Asia and the Pacific was as bleak. The Japanese not only attacked but they successfully took Hong Kong, Wake Island, Singapore, Bali, Burma, and the Philippines. The Japanese were threatening Australia and even Alaska. The only small US successes were a bombing raid against Tokyo and other parts of Japanese home islands, the Battle of the Coral Sea, and the Battle of Midway, an American naval victory over Japan at Midway, west of Hawaii.

The west coast of the United States was bracing for invasion as thousands of Japanese-Americans were being rounded up and sent to internment camps.

This slightly more detailed letter lead with personalized stationary. "SGT. HARRY GREISSMAN" stands out boldly on the top left-hand corner. He complains about the Carolina heat, but not for himself.

A new training cycle has brought 35–45 year olds from N.Y.—mostly business-men, some with families—they really suffer in the sun—110° or more when we drill them—and don't think we don't feel it—but I'm a "veteran" now, aren't I?
Tempis fidget!

Another Harryism.

In this next letter, for the first time we see Harry's response to anti-Semitism, but not any he faced. He read an article in the *Washington Times-Herald*. "Isn't that a Hearst rag," he asks. *"I mean malicious slander on the* Jew *that is Winchell—speaks of his 'base origins' and 'vulture-like antecedents.' Free press, Hah!"* Then he speaks of Frances, from Belgium, whom he had added to his *"lengthy correspondence circle"* and who writes a *"darned good English for a refugee—my French and German pale by comparison."*

Most Americans, more than seventy-five years later, can't really appreciate the effects of Pearl Harbor. We live in a time where warfare is limited to antiterrorist operations. Our most recent traditional wars in Iraq and Afghanistan required only a portion of our now all-volunteer army. The numbers say a lot.

The draft and undrafted enlisted men swelled the army. In 1940 the regular Army numbered 243,095. By July 1941, 606,915 men were inducted into the Army. In December

1941 the Army grew to 1,657,157 and by December 1943 to 5,400,888.[37] There was nary a family left intact. Every family was affected, and worried.

This included, in June 1942, Harry's brother Sol Greissman who enlisted as an apprentice seaman at the age of 24. He became a radioman and served stateside in Boston, Atlantic City, and Southampton, New York, before being transferred to the USS *Peterson*, and USS *Poole*, coast guard destroyers whose main role was to protect cargo and troop convoys in the Atlantic. The *Peterson* had escorted 11 convoys within 19 months during the war and was hit by a hurricane.[38] According to his discharge papers that included his active service record, Sol served through January 31, 1946.

Pearl Harbor also profoundly changed American industry. The Depression finally came to an end. Factories started to produce mass quantities of armaments. President Roosevelt set staggering goals for the nation's factories: 60,000 aircraft in 1942 and 125,000 in 1943; 120,000 tanks and 55,000 antiaircraft guns in the same time period. Others, like the automobile industry, were transformed completely. In 1941, more than 3 million cars were manufactured in the United States. Only 139 more were made during the entire war.

Shipyards turned out tonnage so fast that by the autumn of 1943 all Allied shipping sunk since 1939 had been replaced. By the end of the war, more than half of all industrial production in the world would take place in the United States. While 16 million men and women marched to war, 24 million more moved in search of defense jobs, often for more pay than they previously had ever earned.[39]

On the west coast, in the name of national defense, occurred one of the most infamous racist actions in the history of the United States. To ostensibly to protect our pacific coast from sabotage and spies, over 125,000 Japanese Americans were "relocated to internment camps.

Relocation was, ironically, the word used as well by Germans as they moved Jews to ghettos and camps primarily in Poland. Japanese-American communities saw evacuation orders posted giving them instructions on how to comply with the "relocation orders." Many Japanese-American families, as did German Jews, sold their homes, their stores, and most of their assets at pennies on the dollar. They could not be certain their homes and livelihoods would still be there upon their return.

Ten camps were finally completed in remote areas of seven western states. Housing was mainly tarpaper barracks. Families dined together at communal mess halls, and children were expected to attend school. Needless to say, it was a huge blight on American history.

http://oberlinlibstaff.com/omeka_hist244/exhibits/show/japanese-internment/
government-notions

Fubar (Fucked Up Beyond All Recognition)

On February 4, 1943, Harry was officially designated for active duty. Harry, like so many other veterans before and after him, remained virtually silent until his death about his activities during the war. No doubt he suffered from the depression and guilt that most combat veterans suffer through: survivor's guilt, some version of PTSD, nightmares. His combat and post-combat story until his discharge in January 1946 is based on whatever papers and letters we have found and the history of his units.

Harry had always been in good shape, so the report of his physical examination attached to that letter was no surprise. Lt. Greissman was fit, 26 years of age, had had the usual childhood diseases, and had a "broken upper left hand in 1936" as well as a "Radial Nerve Injury with a slight residual weakness and atrophy of the left hand with complete functional recovery." That was the mysterious injury Harry had mentioned in earlier letters. We believe he was in a car accident. He had perfect vision and hearing, had four molars extracted and was missing two other teeth. He was 5'6 1/2" inches tall and weighed a strapping 130 pounds. His sitting heart rate was 72 and his blood pressure was normal at 120/70.

In a letter from the Field Artillery School's Commandant at Ft. Sill, Oklahoma, Harry was notified of his status as 2nd Lt. Harry Greissman, AO 1176986 and his assignment to "A" Battery, 903 Field Artillery Battalion (FA BN), 78th Infantry Division stationed in Camp Butner, North Carolina, where he was to report by February 18, 1943. As was the custom, Harry went home for what he and his family hoped was not the last time.

Along with the lists of assignments, his particular orders and the health report was included *a* "Pay Guide for Officers, Army Nurses, and Warrant Officers on Change of Station" that came from none other than General George C. Marshall, Chief of Staff, and "Instructions Applicable to Casual Officers Ordered Overseas" that apparently came from no one in particular.

The most important piece of Army bureaucracy in the former was:

> *3. Mailing of paychecks.—The name and address of the bank in which the officer desires his check to be deposited, or the address to which the check should be mailed, must be clearly shown on the officer's pay voucher (item 16); and if to a government office, the office building, and street number should be shown.*

No doubt that piece of information was the only one these newly minted officers paid attention to! The "Instructions Applicable to Casual Officers Ordered Overseas" was filled with information of varying degrees of significance, redundancy, and I would guess humor. I know they had to laugh at some of them, as did I.

First the important: *"Officers, warrant officers, and nurses will be limited to the following (not to exceed 175 lbs. in all)."* Good thing they weren't flying coach today. The baggage was to include:

> *One Musette bag (back pack now)*
> *One piece of hand baggage (not over 40 lbs.)*
> *One bedding roll (not over 50 lbs.)*
> *One trunk locker*

Other instructions involved packing important things in the musette and hand baggage, plainly marking each with one's name and rank; taking two pair of glasses if needed with a prescription entered on immunization forms (Were there opticians on the front?); getting physicals and vaccinations (again); providing emergency addresses (uh-oh); getting pay allotment and insurance straightened out (no kidding); and, obtaining foreign currency. *(Excusez-moi Madame, combien pour une croissant?)* Most serious were the instructions about safeguarding military information that translated into "loose lips sink ships."

"Personnel participating in War Movements" were:

- *"responsible that information concerning the destination, port of embarkation, or sailing date is not discussed with or allowed to reach persons whose official duties do not require knowledge of the movement."*
- *"will not, while enroute from one station to another, communicate by telephone, mail, radio, or telegraph, with anyone, except as may be necessary to the administration or successful completion of the movement.... Personal communications will be collected and also dispatched when the movement involved has been completed."*

Other "interesting" instructions included:

- *"Animals and privately owned cameras will not be taken aboard transports. Radios and electric razors will not be used aboard transports."* (Were the animals publicly owned?)
- *"When boarding transports, individuals will have in their possession gas masks and steel helmets."* (Don't leave home without them, duh!)

And finally

- *"Dependents will not accompany officers."* (Was anyone interested in having his wife and kids being shot at?)

When Harry arrived at Fort Butner, North Carolina, he found a relatively new training facility. Camp Butner, about 28 miles from Raleigh, North Carolina, had opened in August 1942. The camp was built to handle 40,000 soldiers. The Army built row upon row of two-story wooden barracks, as well as three swimming pools, several theaters, and five all-faith chapels. There were several artillery ranges, as well as a prisoner of war camp for Italian and German soldiers.[40]

FROM HERE TO ETERNITY

On the back of one of his IDs we found this:

For a moment of time my world stood still—and listened to the beat of my heart, like a Tom Tom sounding some strange unconsciousness of shadows and swaying pulses. You over there—and you were gone ... and they rocked, on in a still stranger silence

Who did he meet? Who struck him so? Who stimulated that verse?

As it turned out, being stationed near Raleigh was a significant event in Harry's life. It profoundly changed him. One August evening, Harry, like a lot of Camp Butner soldiers, went to Raleigh for a USO dance at Memorial Auditorium. Also at that dance was an 18-year-old college senior named Anne Hetrick of Raleigh, "a standout in her loveliest ball dress and her brown hair curled around her face"[41]

Although Anne first liked another GI named Harry more, she preferred Harry Greissman, the one who she said, "could make words sing."[42] And that he did in many letters written starting when Anne returned to Winthrop College in Rock Hill, South Carolina, and ending over fifty years later when Harry passed away in 1997. These letters were, for a while, in a collection at the North Carolina Museum of History.[43]

Anne was Harry's first real love and many of the letters clearly show that. On September 10, 1943, he writes, after discussing how good it was being Officer of the Day on the day his unit scored 98 out of 100 on a training exercise,

I love you, my darling, love you more than anything this life can offer, and never want to leave you—but if I ever have to go across and face the real thing, I'd want

to go with this gang of ours- and it's a good feeling to know they think the same of
me. I NEVER want to rise so high that I lose sight of their feelings.

At Butner, the officers of the 78th were assigned to train other troops. So Harry became a teacher. Perhaps this assignment became the spark for his love of teaching later in life. The assignment also saved him and his gang from the horrors of war they missed prior to being sent overseas late in 1944.

Harry took advantage of staying stateside by being visited by Anne, and enjoying some old-fashioned home cooking when he visited her at her mother's house. It was customary for families who lived nearby the stark barracks of the army camps to invite GIs for home cookin'.

Apparently, Anne's mom, Ida, even trusted Harry enough to escort her back to college or visit her (chaperoned, of course, by Aunt Kate). When asked if she allowed Harry "liberties" (holding hands) while on liberty, she replied, "of course I didn't…. They were such innocent times."[44]

Harry wanted to be a writer. Harry hoped of becoming a newspaper or sports reporter when his army stint was over, so in one letter 2 weeks later he wrote Anne that he and his buddies went to the movies to see James Cagney in *Johnny Come Lately* a movie that "drives home the place of an honest newspaper in a small town, its place a pleader of causes, some lost, some won, but all bravely fought." Was he thinking of settling down one day in Anne's small town?

But in September 1943, one could not escape the rumors.

> *This place is ominous with rumors…. I hate rumors because I have seen them turn*
> *too many good outfits into spiritless cliques worried about what may come.*

After more months of training at Camp Butner, the 78th was sent for war games in Tennessee. While in Tennessee, on leave in Nashville, Harry once again wrote a series of letters to Anne.

One described Nashville as being a

> *nice town in normal times but right now … it is so overrun by soldiers that the civil-*
> *ians simply stay off the streets … everybody [in the officers' club] drunk on bootleg*
> *gin, so I dropped out. Haven't reached that stage yet.*

A second describes a maneuver "battle" fought on the raging Cumberland River, engorged by a huge storm that swept away many pontoon bridges built by the engineers. He was an umpire of these maneuvers, and part of

> *one of the few outfits to make the crossing and we were a pretty soaking wet band*
> *when we landed on the banks of the Cumberland, far, far away … a realistic replica*
> *of what the 5th Army had to do in Italy many, many times over.*

Soon after he wrote another note saying he could not write for five days, the time required for his next march to his next destination (additional preparation at Camp Picket Virginia?).

In that letter he tells a story only Harry could tell.

> *By the way, darling, did you notice the new point on my pen? Yesterday I managed to steal time to take a haircut in a real civilian barbershop, and while he was clipping my hair, the barber recited the sad tale of a soldier trying to work his way home on a furlough, with a pen as his only asset. The kindly barber gave the GI $4 for his pen, and then recalled his own illiteracy. He tried to trade the pen in for a shovel, and failing that, decided to sell it. So in the process of being clipped about the scalp, I emerged with a new pen but with the same old scrawl.*[45]

Camp Picket was a staging area where the Army readied troops to go overseas. Many privates from the 78th were transferred to divisions that would land in Normandy on D-Day on June 6, 1944, or siphoned off as replacements in outfits already at war in Italy, but luckily, Harry and other officers remained to train more troops.[46]

Harry's prophecy, *"About this talk of going to Officer's training school—That is out completely."* never came true. What effect did these series of events have on Harry's prediction of not becoming an officer? In October 1942, Harry had completed a one-month preparatory course for field artillery officer candidates. After completing Officer Candidate School at Fort Sill, Oklahoma, on February 4, 1943, Harry was made a 2nd Lieutenant. So much for best made plans.

Harry, front and center!

War had something to do with that.

War changes men. Harry, the mild-mannered writer and Renaissance man now had to be more than just proficient at math and physics to be part of a high-efficiency killing machine. Harry was sent to Field Artillery School at Fort Sill, Oklahoma. How do artillery shells land where you want them? He now had to study like he had never done before.

The basic course's scope included: field artillery tactics, administration, combat orders, maps and map substitutes, logistics, reconnaissance, and fire direction (observed and unobserved).[47]

Note the lieutenant's bar and the artillery
insignia on the collar.

The following, from Harry's archives, are some of the artillery notes he took from that course. He may have used the specialized protractor on real combat missions.

I tried deciphering that. As they used to say in my old neighborhood, "Fuggetaboutit!"

Harry went on to use that knowledge as a member of the 78th Infantry Division in Europe.

TO WAR[48]

Harry and the 78th embarked from New York on October 14, 1944.

Dearest Anne, We are bounding along the main ... I'm in the officers lounge now and someone is playing "As Time Goes By" on the piano. He does not play very well, but the haunting strains of the song blend like flying phantoms with the roll of the ship. As time goes by, the tide carries us all farther and farther from the things each of us loves best—and yet the tides were with us long enough for each of us to have lived and loved a little lifetime of reality. You see, it's quite impossible to write without a conscious feeling that the things we used to do and love so well are now being taken care of by others. If distance lends enchantment, it also lends forgetfulness, which is sometimes sweeter than remembering and always healthier than regret ...[49]

TISSUE TIME-OUT! If those words aren't singing, I don't know what would.

They arrived in England on October 26, 1944, and after even more training Harry finally arrived in France on November 22, 1944, where they landed at the port of Le Havre, sailed down the Seine to Rouen, and convoyed by truck to Hoeselt, Belgium. Yes, they missed D- Day and Operation Warlord, the invasion of German-occupied France that took place on June 6, 1944, in Normandy, France.

By the time they arrived in France more than five months of intense fighting had taken place. The Allied forces (American, British, French, and Canadian along with local partisans and some units in exile from occupied German nations) had doggedly pushed the Germans back from their Atlantic fortress.

But when Harry arrived in France in November 1944, things had changed drastically. The Allies had crossed France and Belgium and were virtually knocking on Germany's front door.

On November 28, 1944, the 78th was assigned to XIX Corps, Ninth Army, 12th Army Group.

What does that all mean? The 78th was composed of the following:

- 309th Infantry Regiment
- 310th Infantry Regiment
- 311th Infantry Regiment
- 78th Reconnaissance Troop (Mechanized)
- 303d Engineer Combat Battalion
- 303d Medical Battalion
- 78th Division Artillery
- **903d Field Artillery Battalion (105mm Howitzer) … Here's *Harry!***
- 307th Field Artillery Battalion (105mm Howitzer)
- 308th Field Artillery Battalion (105mm Howitzer)
- 309th Field Artillery Battalion (155mm Howitzer)
- <u>Special Troops</u>
- 778th Ordnance Light Maintenance Company
- 78th Quartermaster Company
- 78th Signal Company
- Military Police Platoon
- Headquarters Company
- Band. Yes, a band.[50]

A corps is a military unit usually consisting of several divisions of which the 78th was one. A division is usually composed of 2–4 regiments of 1,000–3,000 infantry (foot soldiers, "grunts") each, and supporting units of specialist battalions of 300–1,000 soldiers.

An army group is a military organization consisting of several field armies, of which the Ninth was one. Get it now? So organizationally, a division is part of a corps, which is part of an army, which is part of an Army group.

Good, now that we are all clear, Harry was to use all that training to successfully make "small, portable" two and a half ton howitzers, fire high explosive, white phosphorus, and smoke shells with a base diameter of about 4 inches, a maximum range of 7 miles (11 km) to a specified target or targets. I'm impressed. Remember this was an arts and letters guy.

Welcome to Europe. Harry and his buddies got there just in time for what they thought was a relatively calm Christmas for wartime. Little did they know that they would be involved in the most difficult American battle of the European war except D-Day: the "Battle of the Bulge."

FORWARD OBSERVER

During the battle, the 78th was headquartered in Rontgen, in the Rhineland. As part of the Ninth Army they were squared off with the German Fifteenth Army, just north of the actual "bulge."

> Maj. Gen. Edwin P. Parker, Jr.'s newly arrived 78th Infantry Division would attack through the Monschau corridor and continue through the eastern edge of the Huertgen Forest. After seizing Schmidt, the division would attack ... dams from the north.[51]

However, things didn't exactly go as planned ...

> In the mist-shrouded early morning of 16 December, Hitler launched the Fifth Panzer Army, the Sixth Panzer Army, and the Seventh Army in a vain attempt to cross the Meuse River, seize Antwerp, and split the Allied front. Soldiers soon called it the Battle of the Bulge, after the salient the Germans made in the Allied lines. Although surprised, the Allies eventually contained the German offensive, but only after much bitter fighting in freezing temperatures.... From 16 December–25 January, in the Ardennes-Alsace Campaign, the Allies fought to contain and then destroy the forces of Hitler's final offensives in the West.[52]

Apparently, although not usually recognized as other "movie famous" units like the 82nd airborne at Bastogne, according to several sources, the 78th was instrumental in stopping the spread northward of the bulge at the two battles for Kesternich, Germany (December 13–16, and January 30–February 1,1945).

Harry was a forward observer, one of the military's most dangerous jobs. He was not seven miles behind the lines. He was one of the artillerymen who directed artillery fire from the front lines. They were with the troops farthest forward in battle and often sent "forward" of said troops as scouts to locate the enemy and call in artillery fire. It was one of the most dangerous jobs of the war. His job was to figure out how to get shells to land where they needed to land while under enemy fire, often while mere yards away from the target.[53]

Harry's writing slowed. Of course, he was far busier now under more dangerous conditions and perhaps he just didn't have the time. More likely is that sweet Harry couldn't bear to write about what he witnessed. This was the beginning of his shutting down lines of communication about what happened to him and his buddies. We have no notes from Harry describing his accounts, but we do have these other tales.

The following is from *Bracketing the Enemy: Forward Observers in World War II*, published by the University of Oklahoma Press. This dissertation was somewhat of a tribute to Donald L. Walker, who served as a forward observer with the 87th Infantry Division, 334th Field Artillery Battalion, during the war in Europe. It tells Harry's story as well.

> *Walker's father, who with a team of soldiers, would radio back target locations with a team of artillerymen who would then call for and adjust fire.*
>
> *Artillery units would then "bracket shots" at targets by firing two shots on the opposite sides, equidistant from the target, then splitting the distance with the third shot to try to hit the target.*
>
> *A 1944 U.S. Army publication declared that in ground combat, "The forward observer is potentially the most powerful individual in the forward area."*

Descriptions of the action Harry was in are based on accounts from *"DIEHARD," History of the 309th Infantry Division* written by Sgt. Thomas P. Lockhart Jr., I Company, 309th Infantry Regiment, 78th Infantry Division[54] as well as other accounts digested on Wikipedia from a number of different sources.

> *Kesternich is a small village, which in 1944–1945 consisted of about 112 houses constructed in a method of timber-frame and stucco construction called Fachwerkhäuser. Poised on top of a spur ridge, the land inside the village along the main east–west road is relatively flat. The land falls off sharply to the north into a gorge known as the Weidenbachtal, and to the south into a gorge called the Tiefenbachtal.*
>
> *To the east, at the end of the village, the terrain slopes down to the Roer river gorge. Surrounding the village along the ridge was a series of small fields divided by the traditional hedgerow of the region. The houses were not tightly packed, but were surrounded by small yards containing many outbuildings and sheds. Defenders inside the village commanded excellent fields of fire.*

The first battle for Kesternich took place from December 13–16, 1944. Harry and the 78th faced twelve inches of snow on the ground from a storm the night before and below freezing temperatures. A thick ground fog permeated the landscape making visibility difficult until mid-day. Where were the Germans? How could you fire against an unseen yet incredibly lethal enemy you couldn't see? No stateside war game could ever recreate the fear and anxiety these rookie warriors now faced.

The attack by the 78th Division on December 13 interrupted Hitler's plans for the northern (right) edge of the Battle of the Bulge. As part of that attack, with the most forward platoons were forward observers like Harry who "called for all supporting artillery within range."

> *They reached the outskirts of Kesternich as darkness fell on 13 December and dug in. However, they were unable to retain their small purchase and withdrew. The advance had gone decently on the first day and optimism for operations on the next day ran high.*
>
> *At 0600 on 14 December the mission to capture Kesternich resumed. All requests to bring artillery fire on the enemy positions were denied for the reason that it was believed that friendly troops from the 2d Battalion, 309th Infantry were in Kesternich. The situation was so fluid that the 309th's commander did not even know whether or not he had any troops within the town (he did not). The 2nd Battalion, 310th Infantry, made no further gains on 14 December, and dug in for the night approximately five-hundred yards west of Kesternich.*

That is important to know. Often soldiers were accidently hit by friendly fire either incorrectly called in by forward observers or inaccurately fired by the artillery. It is hard to understand what being a forward observer is in today's high-tech world. Today, drones and satellites do the observing for us, and smart bombs find their way into open windows to destroy "targets." But in World War II this was a human endeavor that scarred hearts and minds for decades to come.

To his fellow troops, a forward observer could be a hero or villain. Unfortunately, it was mostly the latter, especially in early combat while observers were still relatively inexperienced and "friendly fire" casualties happened far too often. There was a huge difference between getting high scores on routine training exercises in the states and being successful in the traumatic life and death battlegrounds where you witnessed your friends die grotesque deaths or suffer maiming injuries.

Infantry often blamed forward observers when they thought they were being shelled by friendly fire, even if not. Observers were almost always on the defensive. Often, they would have to defend both their coordinates and the authenticity of their radio call in. If the German artillery was still falling, forward observers were often blamed for not calling in the right coordinates to hit them.

> *A coordinated attack to seize the town of Kesternich commenced at 0700 hours on the morning of 15 December. They succeeded until a German counter attack forced them to retreat, with many Americans taken prisoner. Late on 15 December, a counterattack was sent to retake Kesternich and reach any survivors. One officer said later, "Very few men from the [2nd of the 310th] were found in any of the houses, none [of them] were alive."*
>
> *In the end, the men of the 78th captured Kesternich. One GI with the simple statement described the 3 days of fighting, "Kesternich was very bloody." It was a bloody baptism of fire for the green American division. During the seven days of*

fighting for the village between 13 and 19 December, the 78th Infantry Division lost approximately 1,515 dead, wounded, missing and injured, according to the division's records.[55]

Harry was in the middle of this battle, yet told no one in his family. Where exactly was he positioned? Was he in the town? Was he just outside of it watching, yet unable to help?

Many, like Harry, never spoke a word about their experiences.

Some men, like Lt. James R McGhee and Sgt. Paul Butler, did. They, with another officer, were sent to provide forward observation for the 3rd Battalion, 87th division nearby Harry's 78th. A shell exploded very close to McGhee and a shell fragment pierced the holster harness of his .45 caliber pistol. McGhee reattached the holster with a piece of telephone wire.

> *They began shelling us from our right rear as we were attacking across an open field with a few ancient apple trees scattered here and there.*
>
> *Then I accompanied Captain Wall and Sgt. Cutler in a mad dash to a building atop the ridge.*

Here they had a good view of the village of Medelsheim, and using binoculars like Harry's they could see the movement of German troops.

Inside the steeple they saw German observers whose job it was, like theirs, to direct artillery fire to kill the enemy. McGhee was able to direct artillery fire down on those men and Medelsheim, killing many and destroying large portions of the town. This, however, did not stop the Germans from shelling their buddies. They also spotted tanks nearby firing at them, but their goal to stop the "withering machine gun firing" coming from Medelsheim. Sgt. Cutler remembered later,

> *For a nineteen year old to see a town one minute, and the next minute see it obliterated as if a giant foot had stepped on it and crushed it was very exciting, but in retrospect, it caused me to hate war with a vengeance.*[56]

Harry's forward observer binoculars.

Harry both witnessed and caused scenes like that. How devastating must these experiences have been to this gentle, sensitive man, this writer of poetry who made words sing? Nearby, another forward observer "reportedly called for a fire mission and the first rounds began to land on his own men. Before he could lift the friendly fire, E and F Companies began experiencing heavy casualties." Arthur Ridings, a member of F Company recalled,

"There is no way to determine the number of men killed or wounded by our artillery, however, it did play a major part in the disaster that day."[57]

Somewhere in battle Harry was wounded, yet he did not receive a purple heart. That meant he was patched up by a corpsman (medic) and continued to serve without ever getting sent back to a MASH (Mobile Army Surgical Hospital) unit or hospital. We only knew about it because every few months Harry had to go to a podiatrist to have the bottom of his foot scraped. Scar tissue from the wound had to be dug out. Of course, he never told anyone the details except to say it was shrapnel. That could only have happened two ways. Either he was hit while lying prone, or he was blown backward and hit while in the air. Either way, we know only of the wound.

A sensitive young man like Harry dealt with all this by building a wall around him that lasted until his death in 1997. On Christmas, after some of the most brutal fighting in world history, and "somewhere in Germany with the First Army," Harry finally wrote Anne. Until his letters were discovered we never knew of this beautiful story. Note, we read nothing of the mayhem he witnessed.

Dearest Anne,

My darling, I have just heard and seen something that I shall never forget and there is SO much to remember already:

Christmas services in a winter wonderland blanketed with snow and ice, shattered by cannon and small arms fire. Above the cannon's roar and the angry spitfire of machine guns and rifles, you can still hear the still, small voice of an organ piping hymnals forever old and new. It was a congregation that continued to wear steel helmets and side arms, and hand grenades still dangled brazenly from many a shoulder harness—but the Lord surely saw no blasphemy here—a more devout company never came to worship. Many a face was dirty and bearded and eyes gleamed across the organ notes through slits narrowed by nights with little sleep and less rest. And in the gallant company non was more brave than this chaplain, whose name I do not even know, for they tell me he is wherever the fighting is …

The last notes of the last hymn are dying off in the distance now darling, and each of that strange company is now returning to his separate duty, and yet as I too turn away from the heavens to the hell again, I cannot but think that we are all of us alike, the chaplain and the rest, each serving God and country according to the manner set forth by the destiny beyond us all …

TISSUE TIME AGAIN.

Harry wrote Anne often during that winter and spring of 1945, often on scraps of brown paper left by German troops. The 78th was involved in a second battle for Kesternich from January 30 to February 1, 1945. On February 8, it began its meandering way through German towns from Lammerdorf to Wermelskirchen where it arrived on April 15. During these weeks, they faced skirmishes and battles. Some of the troops actually spotted one of history's first jet planes.

While on this tearful trail of towns, Harry, like many others, collected souvenirs like coins, worthless Weimar marks, a belt buckle, a sword, and insignia from German soldiers. Some he kept and some he sent to Anne. And of course he wrote, but not of war.

> *The smell of spring is none too pleasant here darling. The dead, unburied, leave their trace after the thaws. And yes, it is, in places, lovely countryside, the poor pathetic tragedy of a people without a soul. In their homes are splendid icons, painting of Christ and divine spectacles, in their hearts the hatred that is the only plausible cause for these generations of hell on earth. For their hypocrisy, one can only hate them and wish them nothing but the worst, in this world and the next. But don't let me speak of things like that ...*

Harry's end of the war was difficult to trace. He sent postcards from various places including one from Holland and another Merry Christmas from the continent of Europe 1944 card depicting snowballs being thrown at a snowman Hitler. Letters to family, friends, Anne, and even her mother are postmarked from the First Army APO (Army Post Office) in New York even though he was still in Europe.

There is a photo of him with two other officers taken in Kassel, Germany, in 1945. There is a letter written to Anne on February 12, written from "somewhere in Germany." In it he wonders,

"How much longer can it last darling, or me? It is impossible to write much any more—no place—no time—no lights—not even candles."

Finally, on May 7, German forces unconditionally surrendered. The war in Europe was over. The problem was that there was still a war going on in Asia and many men feared the worst.

Harry's 78th path.

In fact, preparations were being made for many divisions, including the 78th, to be shipped out to fight the Japanese. Fortunately for them, the Japanese surrendered in August. Thank God, many thought, they were now going to go home at last.

Until the end of May, the 78th was assigned to protect a security zone where they cleared towns and wooded areas, and guarded prisoners of war. During this time recreation plans abounded. After the horrors of war, these men deserved time for themselves. Softball and football leagues were created. Physical fitness replaced training and enduring. Healthy inter-army rivalries flourished.

Harry did not go home. Some individuals with special skills like Harry were sent to Berlin to be part of the occupying force in the German capital city. Harry, it turns out, was sent there and wherever else necessary, because of his writing ability and fluency in German. He ended up reporting events for a US army newspaper as well as translating German documents and helping in the interrogation of former German officers and German refugees.

ASSUME THE POSITION

Fearing a future confrontation with Stalin's Soviet Union, there was an effort by the Army to acquaint US troops with the USSR. One effort was a "restricted" ETO (European Theater of Operations) publication called *Army Talks,* Vol. III, No. 3, 20 Jan. 1945 that I found among Harry's possessions. Each of these pamphlets was distributed by order of General Eisenhower himself. Eisenhower's purpose was to:

> *give the soldier psychological preparation for combat, and a better realization of the import of every phase of his military training. Emphasis will be placed on combat orientation. The mental and physical conditioning of the enemy and a proper evaluation of the enemy's weapons and fighting qualities will be stressed. A better understanding of the background of the war, and the soldier's responsibilities in the post war world will also be developed.*

This small pamphlet was all about the USSR, with a subtitle of "How to Blunt Blitzkrieg." It doesn't take much to see what Eisenhower was implying with the publication of this particular volume. It also included combat tips and, on the back page, news from the Pacific.

Although there was good news about the victory in the Philippines, there was bad news about the Japanese ability to defend its homeland. As the troops read this were they now thinking they would have to go up against the Soviets next? Were they going to have to go attack Japan?

Another document was published just a few days before the war ended. This pamphlet titled: *Intelligence Bulletin,* Vol. III, No. 9, May 1945, told them what to envision next. The pamphlet was filled with vivid descriptions of Japanese tactics during recent battles against them in Burma, on Iwo Jima, and in the Philippines, complete with photographs and drawings of Japanese weapons, warning signs, and defense fortifications that GIs might have to face when they were shipped to the Pacific.

That picture was worth a thousand words.

There was also a chapter devoted to German tactics and German analysis of the Allied military. I guess Harry must have smiled when he read these comments on page 47: "Allied artillery merits the highest praise." And, "Observation by spotting aircraft and forward observers is incessant and complete."

Finally, the last chapter is devoted to the Red Army, with sections about "The Man and his Motherland," insignias, and various Soviet tactics. Reading this, what was a GI to think? Were they ever going home?

In April 1945, Harry received a letter from Sam Kaiser of Warner Brother Pictures in New York. Curiously this is the only letter I found addressed to Harry. Sam says, "So you asked the 'four questions' in Herr Goebbels' mansion! Swell Work!!" This was sent the month before the Germans surrendered. Goebbels did indeed have a summer mansion in the woods about 45 minutes north of Berlin. Sounds like Harry may have been there during the Jewish Passover holiday.

> *Don't know which four questions you asked Seder night—the four folks are asking over here are 1) When are the Yanks and the Ivans going to meet? 2) What are they going to do with the Nazi war criminals? 3) How successful is the San Francisco affair going to be? And 4) How much longer before the Nips capitulate?*

The four questions refer to the four questions the youngest asks during the Jewish Passover Seder. These four particular questions are of tremendous importance. Everyone was speculating about the end of the war. The Allies were squeezing Germany's forces and surrounding them. What would happen to Europe? Yes, we knew of the Nazi atrocities. The San Francisco affair refers to the meeting that will eventually set up the United Nations. And of course, would more American soldiers die fighting the Japanese?

The letter was written just after President Roosevelt died and Harry Truman became president. Sam now goes on. "What about Truman? Is Roosevelt's great work going to be for naught?" Truman was a mystery, and people wondered about the abilities of the former haberdasher. In the rest of the letter Sam laments about all the possible consequences, thinks Truman will follow Roosevelt's wishes, and says that,

> you fellas ought to be assured on these points by someone close enough to home to see which way the wind is blowing. [He worries about] the ghosts of [Thomas] Prendergast, the KKK, [as well as the] general nobody knows character of the new chief executive.
>
> Salud, Sam K.

Somehow, Harry was present at a trial that apparently took place in Kassel, Germany, a heavily bombed remnant of the city the British used as a target in retaliation for the German bombing of Coventry, England. His role at the trial was unclear. As an officer he could have been a judge of the accused, an officer prosecuting or defending the accused, or because of his fluency in German, an interpreter when needed or, as a reporter for the *Forward Observer*.

Harry kept a photograph of himself and two other officers, notes on small scraps of paper, and a map that he drew regarding the trial. The photo shows Harry with fellow officers Harrison and Ward, to whom he gives thanks in one of his notes.

The scribbled notes:

- Interviewed from *Neiderhulze (Lower wood): Frau Englbach wife of Ort Gruppen- leiterin: (local team leader) and Frauds Kaerper and Ertzel*
- *NEED: for trial at 18:30*
  - *Thanks to Ward, Harrison, Stark and Gardner, Gardner as witness*
  - *Officer or NCO in charge*
  - *Infantry Capt.*
  - *Black board and chalk*
- *Told him to throw it away*
- *Who's in charge here?*
- *Why are trucks close up so tight?*
- *Harrison: Bottle handed to me*
- *Back of Peabody's?*
- *Describe convoy parked along rd.—Capt. Smith in charge—released in groups*
- *Convoy had been parked one ½ hrs. At this time Tort [the accused] was checking our four trucks had been working on Gardner's truck for 10 minutes before Gen'l*

Greissman, Harrison, and Ward. Harrison, Ward,   Samples of the notes.
Stark, and Gardner seem to have been witnesses.

> *Parker came up; prev had been working on trucks, which had left previously in groups.*

- *Less than one minute before the genl parker approached, Tort heard Ward yell, "Gen'l Parker the 3 girls ..." Went to Stark—girls spoke to Stark about 30 seconds before Gen'l Parker came 5 yards from rest of group but at attention after hearing Ward. Girls ran at this point.*

- *Harrison was holding bottle as if to read label.*

- *Did Parker see girl hand bottle to Harrison?*

- *First knew of bottle was when Gen'l Parker told him to throw it away.*

- *To Tort: Last questions:*

  - *What was first you knew of the three women, the bottle and the Frenchmen?*

  - *What were Gen'l Parker' first words to you?*

  - *Did he refer to the women or the Frenchmen?*

  - *Remind court they were described as German civilians.*

  - *Do you have any previous knowledge or material on this case?*

- *Tort being tried for doing his job at the time he was supposed to be doing it—the same job he had done through garrison and combat. Tort's job: Ass't driver mechanic.*

- *Starkowski:*
  - *3 polish girls*
  - *"Do you speak Polish?"*
  - *30 seconds later here comes Genl Parker*

The General Parker to whom the notes refer was Major General Edwin B. Parker, the commander of the 78th from August 1942 through November 1945.

The last note reflects Harry's judgment about the case, whatever his role was.

- *"The case boils down to this: a Gen'l officer sees 3 girls and a man, nothing more and that's evidence enough for Fraternization. That is, neither law was justice as we read it in books nor promise our men before and after they risk their lives in full performance of their combat duties and on basis of the necessity of executing his job."*

http://www.findagrave.com/cgi-bin/fg.cgi?
page=pv&GRid=37277746&P
Ipi=112022261

On Assignment

At some point someone actually noticed Harry's writing talents. Harry was assigned to be the chief information officer of the *Forward Observer*, the weekly newspaper of the 78th Division. That's a catchy name for a newspaper of an artillery division filled with forward observers. I bet Harry devised it. We don't know when he was assigned, but Harry kept copies from August 15, 1945–November 10, 1945.

When the paper reported the fall of Japan that August the headline was that the surrender was on the eve of the 78th "Lightning's 3rd Birthday."

To keep the GIs informed yet relaxed, the *Forward Observer* read like a college newspaper, like the one Harry was once an editor of, avoiding the big issues at hand—the actual war—and focusing on more pleasing topics like college courses in France, special services shows, interdivisional sporting events, the opening of an officer's sales store. That must have gone over real well with the grunts in the unit.

It also included other features the staff of five designed to take the minds of the troops off the war, including cartoons and editorials, like this (probably written by Harry) from that August 15, 1945, edition:

> *Like his combat counterpart THE FORWARD OBSERVER starts out with an apologia of uncertainty. We earnestly believe that there is a job to be done with an all-Div. Arty weekly that attempts to tie the common interests of four separate battalions into the justly proud unity of "The Lightning Artillery."*
>
> *During the trying winter months from the Siegfried Line to the Seig, every one of us saw and suffered his share of tragedy, hardship, and heartbreak but was there ever one among us who failed to feel the pride and boast of "BATTALIONS WELL MASSED!"; from those in HQ battery, who planned the fires, down to the last lanyard-puller. [The GIs who pulled the lanyard trigger on the howitzers.]*
>
> *No prophet among us has yet come forward to tell us whether or not, or when, we'll get the chance to mass our fires against the sinking Sons of Nippon, but until we do, the Lightning Artillery has been given a wonderful chance to prove we can mass effectively out of the lines as well as in. It's your baby, men … take it from here … and forward is the way.*

Then, abruptly starting from November 17, when the paper's name was changed to *Lightning* and its base of operation changed to Berlin, Harry was no longer listed as information officer. This is when he must have been reassigned to his other, perhaps more secret, duties as an interpreter in interrogations and translator of documents. Many members of the varying regiments that made up the 78th were reassigned and shuffled around. Such is life in the military. He kept *Lightnings* from November 17 to March 30, 1946. Like the *Forward Observer* before it, it was a scrubbed history of the division during that time.

Between his crossing the Belgian and German countryside and the time Harry was sent home in January 1946, he became a collector. Some of what he collected were artifacts of the Third Reich that I was able to use in my tenth grade world history classes so they could understand what Germany was like at the time. I was able to get some of them translated or summarized by a German-speaking student. His astonishment at what he discovered and shared was astounding. Others were quite obvious, even if not translated. They are now at the US Holocaust Museum to be shared with the public.

It seems that many of these could have been possible items in evidence against members of the Third Reich and that Harry translated them for future indictments. But that is supposition. It is just as probable that he collected them as he walked through homes destroyed by the war, vacated by refugees, or as they were searching for the enemy. These were mostly Nazi pamphlets meant to indoctrinate the population.

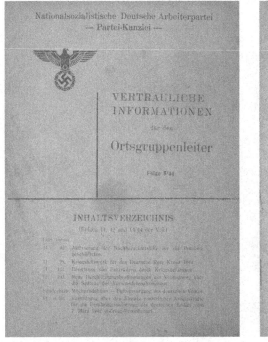

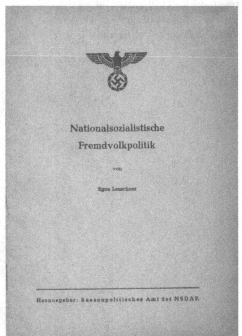

The first of these, however, is a set of instructions. *VERTRAULICHE INFORMATIONEN fur der Ortspruppenlieter, Folge5/44,* translates to: *CONFIDENTIAL INFORMATION for the LOCAL GROUP LEADER. Episode 5/44.* It includes timely details for the end of the war such as: activation of neighborhood assistance for the entered encased bomb, and war welfare organization for the German Red Cross.

Nationalsozialistische Fremdvolkpolitik, the booklet on *Nazi Foreign Policy* is actually about other races in Germany. It helps us understand how and why NAZI policies declared non-Germans as foreigners. It classifies all races as different categories depending on race and color. There are Nordic and non-Nordic people. "German blooded, or not (Jews)." It is against any diffusion of those groups and will try to create an empire only of "Germans."

The above *Guideline for Political Education* is a list of suggested books that present the views of the Nazi Party on topics such as the Fuhrer and the Reich.

The title of this should be clear to all, even in German. *The Jew as World Parasite.*

Now People of this Country, Get Up and Let the Storm (Attack) Begin!
A speech by Dr. Joseph Goebbels given in Berlin in February 1943, three weeks after the tenth anniversary of Hitler taking power and after the huge loss at Stalingrad to bolster enthusiasm after a devastating loss.
"A country that has the strength to take a loss in Stalingrad and is able to gain more power from it, like we did, is undefeatable."

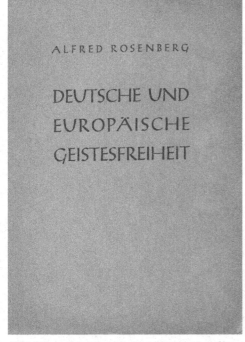

Alfred Rosenberg was the Reich's Minister for the Occupied Eastern Territories. This speech spewing insults about New York and the United States was given in Prague in January 1944.

America as a Perversion of European Culture was published in mid-1942. The first page notes "Reprinting or giving to those who are unauthorized is not allowed." It is amusing, perhaps, to read the author's description of American housewives, whom he thinks can cook only from tin cans.

New York is already the symbol of the city with the least culture in the world. An old German farmhouse has more free religion and spirit than all the skyscrapers and slum barracks combined. Whoever wants religious freedom in the USA will be rolled over. Bach, Goethe, and Beethoven are the best NAZIS ever, because their inner freedom was so great, it will never be achieved again.

The final pamphlet in Harry's possession was this:

Consider it the Nazi Common Core. Here is an example of its "curriculum":

For discussion:

- *"If you attack the party, you sabotage the work of The Fuhrer."*
- *"The enemies are hidden and we have to find them."*
- *"Be active when you talk to Jews; tell them how low they are, and make them feel low."*
- *Why are the Nazis in this war the winners? Because Communism is only talk, the NSDAP works."*

It is a collection of guidelines for schools written
by the National Board of Education.

The last "document" is a bit different.

Adolf Hitler, published in 1936, is a large book sold to families and children. It is a "documentary" to "teach them" about Adolf Hitler by showing him in the best light possible. The most interesting thing is that it is also a photo album that came with spaces to glue in collected photos that could be bought in stores and traded (like baseball cards). The goal was to collect and paste in the set that belonged in the book to illustrate the various friendly faces of the Fuhrer in various places in Germany with various "Volke."

I was struck as to how similar it was to the "picture" books sold in supermarkets when I was a kid in the 1950s, which many American kids collected about places and heroes. Imagine the shock my German-American student had when he translated those. Imagine Harry's shock in 1945 because he could read it fluently in German.

When Harry finally did go home, he brought very little of his military equipment back with him. Of course the Army confiscated his weapons. What remained was his Army jacket, his knife, a sword, a pin from the 78th, and a pair of binoculars he used when he was a forward observer. Looking through those binoculars, I tried to imagine his gentle soul watching unsuspecting German soldiers from a hidden distance, plotting and radioing in the coordinates to send off to his artillery units, then watching as the Germans were blown to smithereens. Is that why he never spoke of the horrors he witnessed? Was it because he felt guilty, horrified at the results of his actions?

This is the one artifact that was always visible at 10 Kenneth Road. As lore has it, a Belgian family grateful for saving them from the German tyrants gave him this.

This hung in Harry's kitchen until he moved. We still have it.
Translated from the Flemish, it means:
The most beautiful name
In all the world
The most name known to
Mankind is: Mother.

We know that at some point in time Harry became a member of both the 78th Division Veteran Association and the Association for Veterans of his 903rd Field Artillery Battalion. He saved copies of *The Flash*, the publication of the 78th Division Association, and newsletters from the 903rd's association. None of them are earlier than 1984. I think he finally did this because we, his family, encouraged him to try to reconnect with former GI buddies. Mostly a collection of updates on the veterans of the 78th, there were occasional photos and stories, but in the only index I could find, there were only five contributions by members of the 903rd.

Only one story, by a Colonel Thurman Irving, in the April 2001 edition of *The Flash* mentioned Harry's "A" battery. Was he still with it at the time this story took place? It was at Remagen Bridge, a major battle in March 1945 when "A" battery lost one killed and four wounded. Irving includes a description of the black market that existed in postwar Berlin.

> *Cigarettes cost 50 cents per carton for the US soldiers and each man received one carton per week as his ration. A carton sold for $100, and up to $200 at Christmas time. Butter sold for $35 per pound; sugar brought $25 per large GI cupful, and wristwatches were $500 TO $3,000. Jeeps sold for thousands of dollars.*

In 2016 dollars those black market cigarettes would sell for approximately $1,300 and $2,600, the butter for $450, the sugar for $330. The watches would range from $6,700 to $40,000. Jeeps? Fuggetaboutit!

Irving's story ends with an experience that may well have been Harry's as well. It describes the division leaving Berlin and traveling back to the United States on a converted cargo ship manned by a crew that included a large number of "fourteen and fifteen year old kids from Brooklyn" who he presumes broke into their luggage. When the weather turned severe and the ship "listed 47 degrees and rocked back and forth at 8 second intervals" no one ate. "Waves flew over the deck. At times the propeller came out of the water."

He feared the ship "would disintegrate." Unable to stay in their bunks, many locked "legs around a steel post" and had to deal with a head (bathroom) filled with vomit that went unclean for the two-week voyage. By the time they cheered the Statue of Liberty and sailed up the Hudson on January 23, 1946, the ship had lost some of its lifeboats and a "huge boom lay amidships." USO dancers welcomed them from the deck of another ship in the river.

The 903rd newsletter tried to keep tabs on members of the association. I found one reference to Harry in the February 1985 edition.

> *Harry Greissman's Jan 17th letter said snow bound at home, and doesn't blame people for retreating to Florida. As he was writing the winds and snow were blowing outside the window. Early in February, he and Iris will start a three-week vacation in the Miami Area. Hoping to get to Ft. Myers, if Iris's brother in Ft. Lauderdale, who had a stroke, would be well enough, so they could continue their trip to the*

west coast. We hope to hear from you. Harry was sorry that he missed the dedication to Gen. Parker. He said that he and Division Artillery Commander were two of his unforgettable combat memories. Both were great men.

In 1970, the 78th Division was recognized in a proclamation and given a "78th Division Day" by then Mayor John V. Lindsay. It said:

> *The 78th Division Veterans Association members served with distinction in two World Wars.*
>
> *World War II veterans of the Lighting Division, which held the line during the Battle of the Bulge, captured the Schwammenauel Dam on the Ruhr River intact; and played a major role at the Remagen Bridgehead.*
>
> *The men of Lightning will gather in our city to pay homage to the comrades who made the supreme sacrifice on the occasion of its silver anniversary reunion.*

We don't know if Harry was at that ceremony. We know nothing more. The only reference we have by Harry of General Parker was in the trial where he thinks the general falsely accused someone of fraternization. Harry, not long after became a snowbird and eventually he and Iris "retreated" to Florida.

CATCH 22

One would think that after five years of service and surviving the horrors of war, the military would make coming home easy for these still suffering vets. But, noooooooo … bureaucracy rules. Just when you think you are going home.…

This Western Union telegram dated 2:16 PM, January 8, 1946, sent to sister Leah Greissman tells the story. By the end of the month Harry had returned stateside, not yet to Brooklyn, but to Fort Dix, New Jersey, from where he would be discharged back to civilian life.

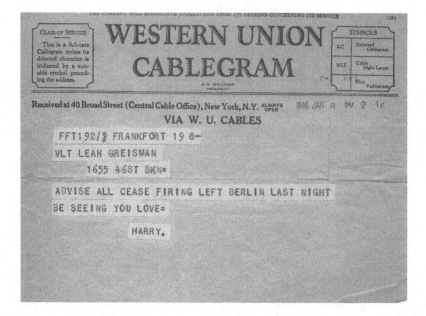

According to special orders number 26 dated January 26, 1946, 1st Lt Harry Greissman (he was promoted again in November 1944) of 1655 46th St. Brooklyn, New York, was to be processed and granted terminal leave. Three days later, came special order number 29. Each of the 38 officers on the list was to become inactive on dates that ranged from February 15 to June 13. Harry's process would take exactly fifty-eight days, and he would "revert to inactive status" on March 29, 1946.

Why two months? Really? During this time there was loads of paperwork to be done.

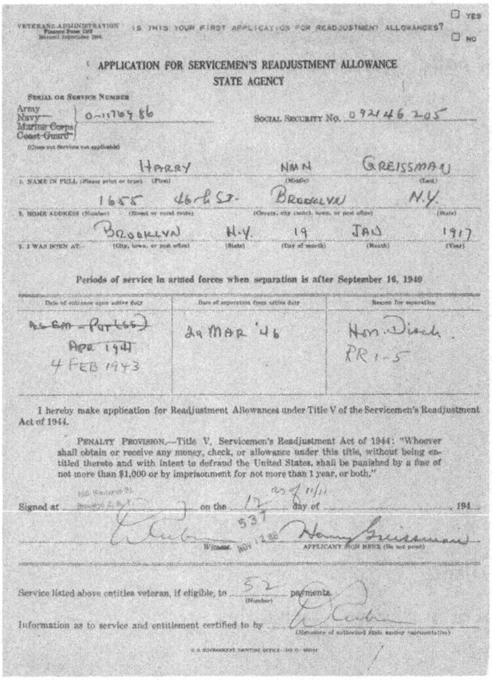

IS THIS YOUR FIRST APPLICATION FOR READJUSTMENT ALLOWANCES? ☐ YES ☐ NO

VETERANS ADMINISTRATION

APPLICATION FOR SERVICEMEN'S READJUSTMENT ALLOWANCE
STATE AGENCY

SERIAL OR SERVICE NUMBER
Army / ~~Navy~~ / ~~Marine Corps~~ / ~~Coast Guard~~ 0-1176486 SOCIAL SECURITY No. 092 46 205
(Cross out Services not applicable)

1. NAME IN FULL (Please print or type) HARRY (First) NMN (Middle) GREISSMAN (Last)

2. HOME ADDRESS 1655 46th ST. BROOKLYN N.Y.

3. I WAS BORN AT— BROOKLYN (City, town, or post office) N.Y. (State) 19 (Day of month) JAN (Month) 1917 (Year)

Periods of service in armed forces when separation is after September 16, 1940

Date of entrance upon active duty	Date of separation from active duty	Reason for separation
~~As EM – (Pvt.)~~ ~~Apr 1941~~ 4 FEB 1943	29 MAR '46	Hon. Disch. RR 1-5

I hereby make application for Readjustment Allowances under Title V of the Servicemen's Readjustment Act of 1944.

PENALTY PROVISION.—Title V, Servicemen's Readjustment Act of 1944: "Whoever shall obtain or receive any money, check, or allowance under this title, without being entitled thereto and with intent to defraud the United States, shall be punished by a fine of not more than $1,000 or by imprisonment for not more than 1 year, or both."

Signed at .... on the 12 day of ...., 194..

Witness .... APPLICANT SIGN HERE (Do not print) Harry Greissman

Service listed above entitles veteran, if eligible, to 52 (Number) payments.

Information as to service and entitlement certified to by .... (Signature of authorized State agency representative)

U.S. GOVERNMENT PRINTING OFFICE

WAR DEPARTMENT
OFFICER'S PAY, ALLOWANCE, AND MILEAGE VOUCHER

WORK SHEET

1. When corresponding with this office, request that you refer to the following items:
(a) Date of Departure from this Station.
(b) Par. No., SO No., & date of Separation order
(c) Date of Reversion.
(d) Full Name, Rank, and Army Serial Number.

Application for serviceman's readjustment allowance. *Officer's pay, allowance, and mileage voucher.*

The figures on the form will add up to Harry's "going away" money accrued from January through May.

Total Credits: $1,017.87

Total debits, Debits? $141.70

Net Balance: $896.17

And thanks again for your service. You would think that after what those poor GIs went through they would be sent home without having to deal with all this crap. Note the index card with specific instructions. I don't know if this was attached to all forms or Harry received it because he botched his first attempt, not unlikely. The front of the card reads:

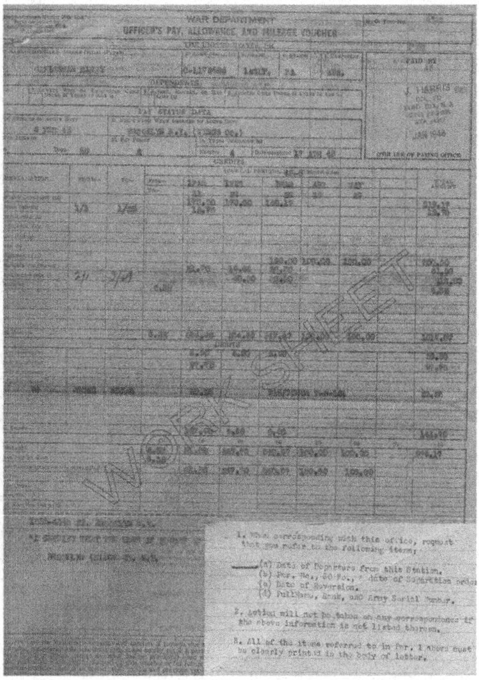

1. When corresponding with this office, request that you refer to the following items:
(a) Date of Departure from this Station
(b) Par. No. So no., & date of Separation order
(c) Date of Reversion
(d) Full Name, Rank, and Army Serial Number

2. Action will not be taken on any correspondence if the above information is not listed thereon

3. All of the items referred to in Par. 1 above must be clearly printed in the body of the letter.

On the back, on the top, in a threatening tone, appears this:

Penalty for private use to avoid payment of postage: $300.00.

A "penalty for private use to avoid payment of postage"—what the?

And, of course, there was the ever important certification letter dated 30 Jan '46, that Harry, as all others to be finally set free, had to sign.

> *I certify, that prior to my departure from Fort Dix Separation Center, Fort Dix, New Jersey, I have returned all government property and equipment issued to me and now in my possession.*
>
> *I certify that, to the best of my knowledge and belief, I have settled all of my financial and property accounts.*

Please drive home safely and come again. Can you imagine being treated that way after dodging bullets, artillery, and God knows what, while seeing your buddies blown up in front of your face?

I assume the officer's pay form accounted for the last document, and I know that Harry, like other soldiers, kept souvenirs like his dagger and binoculars. After being treated like that, I'd have stolen a tank if I could.

It was nice, though, to also get this form letter, "signed" by the president.

To you who answered the call of your country and served in its Armed Forces to bring about the total defeat of the enemy, I extend the heartfelt thanks of a grateful Nation. As one of the Nation's finest, you undertook the most severe task one can be called upon to perform. Because you demonstrated the fortitude, resourcefulness and calm judgment necessary to carry out that task, we now look to you for leadership and example in further exalting our country in peace.

That spring, the Greissman clan could finally reunite before it separated to the various locales each of the siblings would eventually choose to take their families. Solomon and Abraham were discharged from the Coast Guard on January 31, 1946, and March 19, 1946.

How did the army help the former GIs of the "Greatest Generation" when they returned home? It gave them more booklets and documents in a feeble attempt to try to prepare them for peacetime living.

Harry's clearly unused *Going Back to Civilian Life* booklet is a neat little pocket-sized eighty-five-page helpful and cheery guide complete with cute little drawings of smiling soldiers leaving camp, with their happy families, dressing for work, going on an interview, getting medical care, and getting back to work. I am sure he found it childish and unworthy of a mature 30-year-old grizzled veteran. I did when I read it.

Harry's clearly used *The Amended GI Bill of Rights* pamphlet gave a clear and detailed explanation of its provisions, provided frequently asked questions and answers, and for the researcher among them, the actual and complete amended text. Harry and other grizzled veterans did make good use of this extremely practical tool.

But could *Going Back to Civilian Life* or *The Amended GI Bill of Rights* really tell them about readjusting to peacetime life? Could they explain the reoccurring nightmares and the panic attacks? Could they explain what we now know as PTSD and what then was called battle fatigue? Could these pamphlets really help them with "divorces, medical problems, exploding family expenses, and shortages in everything from jobs and housing to reliable automobiles and decent white dress shirts"?[58]

Could these publications and re-indoctrinations they received at their "separation centers" prevent "the behavior of returning veterans, men whom many believed drank away their military separation pay and benefits and spent too much time idling on park benches, [or men] who went away to war young, fresh, and confident and returned nervous, bitter, or plagued by nightmares."[59]

What were Harry's nightmares? He said practically nothing about his wartime experiences, yet kept the treasure trove of material I used to write this. We know that he somehow got his hands on and kept a copy of the *Lightning* dated March 9, 1946, yet still being published in Berlin by those in the 78th who still remained there. Which articles intrigued him? Did something in it tell him about old friends? Was he curious about how life in Germany had changed since he left? Was he trying to find information about long lost European cousins? We don't know. He never said.

And Anne? What about Anne? Could the pamphlets prepare him for …

DEAR HARRY

What we know of Harry's first love is thanks to Anne, Larry King in his book, *Love Stories of World War II*, and Sarah Avery in her 1999 article, "Love Letters," in *The News & Observer* of Raleigh, North Carolina. Many GIs, like Harry, had girls, fiancées, or even wives. Some had already received the dreaded "Dear John" letter, which sadly told them that their former girlfriend, fiancée, or wife had left them for another man.

> *Harry wanted Anne to marry him and that summer she went north to meet his family, staying with his sister, [Dorothy] in Pennsylvania, who was warm and welcoming, as were his other family members.*[60]

In Anne's case, as in the case of so many other young stateside women, absence did not necessarily make their hearts fonder. She began to have doubts. She worried about their differences in religion.

> *Somehow, I just knew it wasn't right. I can't really explain it. But I just knew that for Harry to lead a long and happy life, and for me to lead a happy life, our paths should separate.*[61]

It must have been devastating for Harry. This was his love, his darling, and the woman he corresponded with for so many years through so many difficult times. More than likely he was dreaming of marrying Anne, moving to Raleigh, and becoming a writer for that small town newspaper. How did she say it? How did he react? How did his family help him recover?

All we have is this poetic response from Harry:

Dear Anne,

Sorry to disappoint but Truman is STILL the big surprise of the year. When I came all the way down to Dixie to see you last September, I knew. And now, in

85

November, I know no more than in September. So, all the best, Anne- and it IS the best for you, to be sure.

One day, when the war years become a tattered record in some kid's history book, a soldier that "was" may add a chapter to the story that remains to be told. 'Til that day, you will grow up in the sweet tradition of your noble ancestry—and continue to search for that "something" which lies buried between the gray leaves of memory.

It will, of course, be impossible for me to see the "the last of Miss Hetrick"—but where your good church bells chime out the glad tidings, listen for the whisper of a sigh from the big bad city of the North—and with that whisper will come all the fond hopes and best wishes for the noblest lady I have known.

Always in all ways,

Harry

He knew their cultural differences had become too great. Would her noble ancestry have accepted a Jew in their family? Would his accept a "goy"? His letter reassures her of making the best decision for her. Was he inferring that he would, in some future time, write his story or theirs? There is so much meaning in his phrase, between the gray leaves of memory. Did he mean confederate gray?

Close your eyes and you can see the scenes in the movie. Church bells echo in the North Carolina Blue Ridge hills. Cut to Brooklyn. Harry walks down Fort Hamilton Parkway. He stops. He turns to face southward. He lets out a long slow sigh thinking of his beautiful Anne. Then he gets an egg cream.

In December 1948 Anne married Frank Kennedy, a staff engineer at North Carolina State University. Harry sent a one-word telegram: *"LUCK."* Two years later Harry married Iris Resnick of Brooklyn, his wife until his death forty-seven years later. For those forty-seven years the two couples exchanged Christmas cards. When Harry died, in his wallet was a photograph of a young Anne Hetrick. It rhymes with Resnick.

COMING HOME

We have all seen, read, or heard about veterans returning home from Afghanistan, Iraq, and Vietnam with various issues trying to readjust to domestic life. Stories of PTSD-afflicted veterans haunt us. Back in the 1940s, however, there was no PTSD. Veterans then suffered from battle fatigue. It was not a "psychological condition." They all came home suffering from the experiences of war. They had to adjust not just to peacetime but to a very different nation from the one they left.

Postwar America was in flux. Millions of women laborers during the war returned to their homes as war-weary vets reclaimed their jobs. Cities like New York were more integrated. Between 1940 and 1950 the Black population in New York increased by 285,000. Puerto Ricans came from the island to find new opportunities in New York City. Some of Harry's Brooklyn changed, but not much. Harry returned to still Jewish Borough Park. In 1950, there were almost 2 million Jews in New York City, over 25 percent of the city's 90.2 percent white population. Of that number, 920,000 lived in Brooklyn, still almost 36 percent of the borough's population.[62]

Economically, Brooklyn suffered. At this time, major cities started to lose manufacturing jobs to other locations in the country. Just as huge areas of the Midwest now suffer from loss of factories and jobs now, so did major cities like New York City then. The Brooklyn docks deteriorated as large container ships, requiring deeper harbors, began to dominate the shipping trade. This economic dislocation and the easy availability of government-sponsored GI housing loans spurred the middle classes to leave their old neighborhoods for the suburbs.

The postwar era saw the beginning of the baby boom era. It also brought a huge population shift to the New York suburbs, especially Nassau and Suffolk Counties on Long Island, and Westchester County, just north of the city. The GI Bill of Rights led to the construction of thousands of suburban housing tracts like Levittown in Hempstead, Long island, New York.

White flight started. Hundreds of thousands of white middle-class residents began to abandon Brooklyn and Queens for Long Island, Staten Island, and New Jersey. Whole Jewish communities fled their old neighborhoods and either first moved to Flatbush, Borough Park, Eastern Parkway, Brighton Beach, and Marine Park or directly to new suburbs.[63]

Outside of Brooklyn, the country's economy boomed. Auto manufacturing skyrocketed as suburbs grew everywhere, creating a need for new roads and even more cars. The Eisenhower administration created the Interstate Highway System to encourage mobility and economic growth. That directly impacted Harry because it was the building of Interstate 87 (the New York State Thruway) that led to the development of Huntley Estates, in Ardsley, New York, where Harry moved his family into a brand new split level in 1957, unlike most Brooklyn Jews, who fled east to Long Island.

With the growth of manufacturing came jobs with decent union wages. The GI Bill provided avenues for veterans to build new lives. New families could afford new homes and the goods to fill them. The need for more management positions created more white-collar jobs. The consumption of goods became our economy's goal. Advertising helped consumers "choose" which goods to buy. That would become Harry's occupation.

Harry re-immersed himself into everyday life after serving in the military for four years, being in one of the worst battles of World War II, and losing his dream of marrying Anne. From 1946 through 1950, after his return to Brooklyn, he reconnected with his parents and siblings, started a new job, and met his future wife of forty-seven years. After the war, Harry took a job with a small Brooklyn newspaper. He really wanted to be a sports

The book, *Stork's Eye View of Advertising Men* (1950), was according to the publisher, *Parent's* magazine, "in a lighthearted moment,". might have been on Harry's desk about the time Harry was about to become a father to his eldest son, Richard.

journalist. He loved writing about sports. Instead, over time, he became a pipe-smoking family man in the gray flannel suit, ad man, who worked on some of the accounts depicted on the Emmy-winning TV show *Mad Men.* That 1932 New Utrecht yearbook prophecy had come true, "And Harry Greissman is the publicity agent."

However, there were weaknesses in the postwar and 1950s bubble. We were a very segregated nation. Civil rights violations were everywhere. Lynching still occurred. Jim Crow was a powerful force in the south. Even in northern cities de facto segregation was widespread. Internationally, we faced a new danger, the Soviet Union, and its dictator, Josef Stalin.

Stalin made Putin look like the Easter Bunny. In postwar Europe, the Soviet Union, Stalin's totalitarian communist, command economy, was a far different place than the capitalist democracy of the United States. Differences were too great to overcome. The resulting Cold War would last a half-century. The postwar expansion of the Russians into Eastern European nations was anathema to Americans who had fought for the right of these nations to once again become free states. In Asia, China exited World War II to a continuing civil war between the nationalist forces of Chiang Kai-shek and Communist forces of Mao Tse-tung, (Zedong), with Mao winning in 1949.

In 1945, the United States used two nuclear bombs to defeat Japan. By the early 1950s the Russians had also developed nuclear bombs. Both the United States and the Soviets were stockpiling them as fast as they could to create the means to "deliver them." The two superpowers began the policy of mutually assured destruction (MAD). Don't you love that? They built as many nuclear warheads as possible so no one would be the first to attack. We had entered the Nuclear Age and Cold War era, and that scared most of us shitless.

The mounting fear of the Soviet Union and their development of nuclear weapons led to a rampage against anyone who was suspected of being communist or a lefty sympathizer. Harry had cut out and kept a December 1947 column by notorious right-wing columnist Westbrook Pegler. Harry would have hated Pegler. This "Red Scare" somehow concerned Harry.

> *The House Committee on Un-American Activities, led by John E. Rankin of Mississippi used what they called, "a wealth of information that has gone far toward protecting this Nation from saboteurs of all kinds" to attack those they perceived to be "communists or communist supporters." At the height of the Cold War rivalry between the United States and the Soviet Union, HUAC's influence soared and contributed to a climate of domestic fear stoked by its sensational and often unsubstantiated investigations.*[64]

Pegler disparaged Franklin Delano and Eleanor Roosevelt, the New Deal, labor, intellectuals, poets, and radicals. Pegler could have been Donald Trump's PR guy. He would cheer on lynch mobs as he did in 1936, or "exhort solid citizens to join strikebreakers 'in the praiseworthy pastime of batting the brains out of pickets.'" In time, he would stake Red Scare leader Senator "Joe McCarthy to a run with relentless good press."[65]

In the column *"Comments on Trends of Movie Red Probe,"* Pegler ripped a new movie, *Body and Soul* because it has in it a "Negro actor," Canada Lee, who

Since he took to speaking recitations with expression and gestures he developed some-thing called social consciousness. His name bobs up again and again in the company of other names often cited by the Committee on Un-American Activities.

Then he rips Enterprise Studios and David Hopkins. Why? Because David is

little Davey, the son of the late Harry "Rasputin" Hopkins, the man who came to din-ner in the White House and remained as the guest of the U.S.A. for years and years.

Harry Hopkins was one of FDR's closest advisors. Rasputin was a Russian mystic and most trusted friend and advisor to the last Russian czar and his family.

But why was Harry so interested in this particular column. Reading further one discovers why. In the attack on little Davey, Pegler attacks a "South American coffee cartel, Eleanor Roosevelt, and the Buchanan Advertising Agency." He also mentions the Kudney Ad Agency. Did Harry know people at these agencies? Was he contemplating working there? Who did Harry know? Was he worried that he might be investigated or that he was a friend with or associated with people who were? The fear was real. These were signs of the times. The Red Scare and hunt for "communists or communist supporters" went on for virtually a decade, most notoriously led by Senator Joe McCarthy.

Thousands were blacklisted including Helen Keller, Pete Seeger, Leonard Bernstein, Zero Mostel, Charlie Chaplin, Langston Hughes, Danny Kaye, Lena Horne, Gypsy Rose Lee, Burgess Meredith, Ruth Gordon, Eddie Albert, and Dalton Trumbo.

The Federal Loyalty-Security Program, created in 1947, gave loyalty review boards the power to fire federal employees when "reasonable grounds" existed for belief that they were disloyal. In practice, people could lose their jobs for being on the wrong mailing list, owning suspect books or phonograph records, or associating with rela-tives or friends who were politically suspect. Those accused almost never learned the source of the allegations against them.

    McCarthy had become the most feared and perhaps most powerful man in America. McCarthy cared little about the accuracy of his accusations, and he made heavy use of intimidation and innuendo. Nevertheless, his complete disregard for the truth only made him more powerful and frightening. Few dared to challenge McCarthy directly, and many Republicans who despised him found him useful. (Pres-ident Eisenhower told aides that he would not "get into the gutter with that guy.")[66]

Another fear of former GIs like Harry was the "hot" war in Korea that started two weeks after Harry and Iris wed. Harry was 35. He, Iris, and both their families worried he might be recalled. As it turned out, he wasn't. The war began after North Korea, backed by the Soviets and Communist Chinese, attacked South Korea, supported by the United States and its allies. This "proxy" war between the "forces of international communism" and the "forces of Democracy" included American troops from July 1950—July 1953, when the war ended as a stalemate. A stalemate? Over 33,000 American servicemen lost their lives. Another 92,000 were wounded. But it all turned out okay for Harry and his new family.

WHEN IRIS
MET HARRY

Back in Brooklyn after the war, Harry was getting back to normal. He reconnected with his brother Sol and his friend Paul and got back to playing his beloved tennis, even, according to the photo that follows, in the cold.

About the time he lost Anne to Frank Kennedy, Harry met Iris Resnick through a friend of his brother Jack's wife, Rose Greissman. Rose was friends with Iris's much older sister Ruth Resnick Gould with whom she was living in Brooklyn. Rose and Ruth knew each other because they both went to Pine Lake Park, a bungalow colony in what may have seemed way upstate to Brooklynites, but was in what became suburban northern Westchester County. It was conveniently located in Cortlandt Manor, near enough to the commuter train station in Peekskill, New York, so dads could commute.

Bungalow colonies were a staple of Jewish New York middle-class existence at that time. What's a bungalow? The term was derived from a British Empire legacy, from a Bengali word meaning "low house."[67] They were small two- to three-room houses with few frills, just basic amenities, with a screened-in porch to sit free of insects on hot summer nights.

Bungalows were not only refuges from the hot steamy city streets, they provided an escape from the anti-Semitism many residents faced at work or on the teeming streets of the city. Many Jews still faced barriers at work either getting a job or earning promotions. Many college-aged Jews could not go to the top schools that closed their doors to them. Most resorts, clubs, as well as workplaces were closed to them.

Starting as early as the 1880s Jews bought land upstate, ranging from northern Westchester where Pine Lake and other enclaves grew, northward to the Catskill Mountains, to what eventually became known as the "Borscht Belt" or the "Jewish Alps."

During the 1920s and 1930s northern Westchester County and the Lower Hudson Valley also became home to summer and full-year enclaves built by socialists/workers communities like the Workman's Circle. The Workman's Circle established a Jewish lodge and Camp Kinder Ring, in Duchess County in 1926 where two of Harry's grandchildren, my kids, eventually went. Close to Pine Lake was the Mohegan Colony, "a cooperative community that served as an experiment in egalitarian living and child rearing."[68]

Nearby lived famous left-leaning celebrities like L. Frank Baum, the author of *The Wizard of Oz*, along with singer/songwriters Woody Guthrie, and Pete Seeger. The surrounding area was not entirely enthralled. In fact, a year before Harry married Iris, there was a huge riot when it was announced that another famous "lefty," Paul Robeson, was to do an open-air concert. Remember this was the Red Scare era and Paul Robeson was also a black man.

> *The demography of Peekskill and its neighboring northern Westchester Hudson River communities was mixed, even schizophrenic. On the one hand, there were the summer people and weekenders, many of whom were middle-class Jews with left-of-center leanings. On the other hand, there were the year-round residents, more working class and conservative, whose resentment, and even open hostility to the "summer people" had been steadily growing.*[69]

On the night of August 23, 1949, a mob formed to harass concertgoers. Were any Greissmans or Resnicks there? Veterans groups paraded. Car horns blared. Patriotic bands played.

> *Attackers screamed: "We're Hitler's boys—here to finish the job." The mob swelled to over a thousand. A twelve-foot high cross was burned. Books and sheet music were burned ... while the performers and concert-goers, arms linked together, sang such songs as "The Star-Spangled Banner," "God Bless America" and "Solidarity Forever." The concertgoers, artists and organizers tried to defend the concert site, but by the time the evening was over, every defender had been injured.*[70]

Two weeks later there was another concert. Following the concert, the police apparently tried to safeguard those who went by routing the vehicles up a steep, long, and winding road through the northern Westchester County woods. However, the convoy found the road blocked by a mob that hurled rocks at the more than fifty buses and countless cars. All had their windows smashed. At least fifteen cars were overturned. Bus drivers abandoned their vehicles and fled on foot, leaving about a thousand of their passengers stranded.

Years later Seeger reported he met a man who told him what his dad, a local police officer at the time admitted to him,

> *You know, that riot was all arranged by the Ku Klux Klan and the police.... They had walkie-talkies all through the woods. They had that place surrounded like a battlefield.*[71]

Such was life for Jews in the "liberal" New York metropolitan area.

Anyway, according to her niece June, who looked up to her as an older sister and apparently made quite a lot of money earning quarters to "disappear," Iris was a quite beautiful woman who had many suitors. Ruth and Iris were seventeen years apart. Their mom died at the young age of 49, and because their father, Louis, ran a bar, and was often away at night, Iris moved in with Ruth, her husband Joe, and their children Arnie and June. At first Iris and Arnie shared a room while they lived in Borough Park. Don't be shocked. That was once very common when families were too large for their dwellings. As she required more privacy, Iris was given the living room.

Since Ruth raised Iris, they maintained closer contact than most sisters. As a result, there was an extraordinary closeness between Iris, Harry, Ruth, and Joe. Many thought Joe and Harry were brothers. This closeness was passed down to Harry and Iris's nephew and niece, Arnie and June, and in time to his daughter Jamie, who became very close to her "older sister" June. Harry taught Arnie tennis on visits to Pine Lake and took him to play back in Brooklyn.

Iris was 21 when she married 35-year-old Harry. Young by today's standards, that was two years older than the norm for women in 1950. Harry was thirteen years older than the average age for men to get married, which was 22. Today those ages are 27 and 29. Then, it was old even for a World War II vet. According to June, Iris's "men" were all adorable boys. Harry was the "first man," much older and more sophisticated than any of the others who came calling.

June recollects,

> *He spoke several languages, was making approximately $20,000 [she thinks] a year, [worth about $200,000 in 2016 dollars] and was clearly in a different category than the rest of her boyfriends. He gave her what was then considered a very large diamond, and she was entranced."*

They played tennis together. Harry called Iris "a natural on the court." According to June, they seemed to have a perfect life. Iris was swept off her feet. It must have worked out well because they married on June 11, 1950. Their marriage would last until Harry's death in 1997.

The bride and groom.

Jack escorts Harry down the aisle. Check out the fedoras. Hipper than a yarmulke.

This picture contains most of Harry's relatives at the time.
Front row, left to right: Unknown, Edie and Judie, Jack's daughters
Middle row: Jack's wife Rose, Aaron, Mary, Iris, Harry, sister Leah
Rheingold
Back row: Brothers Sol, Jack, and Louis and his wife Anita;
brother Abe, sister Frieda (Fritzy) and her plus one; sister Dorothy
and her "weird" husband, Jack Israel.

Iris and Harry married June 11, 1950. Richard was born on March 10, 1951. Do the math. They must have really enjoyed their honeymoon at Green Mansions in Lake George. It must have included more than just tennis, fireplaces, and boating.

"Green Mansions operated from 1922 to 1965 as a 'summer only' resort, featuring Adirondack lodging, dining, athletics and entertainment." It is now open as a full-year *"modern, leisure home community"* where families can either buy or rent homes.
http://www.adirondackcondos.com/lake-george-ny-mountain-rentals.html

BACK IN BROOKLYN

Their new home, at East 36th Street and Avenue U, Brooklyn, would become Harry's second home away from his parents, the first being everywhere the army sent him. Their two oldest children, Richard and Jamie, were born here. It was half a block from Marine Park, four miles from where Harry grew up. Many of the houses, single- and two-family homes, were built in the late 1930s. They lived upstairs in a two-family house across from the Bledsoes, who would become lifelong friends. The Bledsoe family included their son Barry, his older brother Kenny, and his grandmother who lived on the top floor. Harry and Iris's son Richard recalls sneaking up the back stairs of closest friend Barry's house into his grandmother's area to scare her. Word has it that they were more scared of her.

Except for the fact that Marine Park was still underdeveloped enough that across the major roadway there were tar pits, and it was somewhat isolated by a lack of subway access, it was a perfect semi-suburban location for the new Greissman family. Once, Richard fell into those pits, waist-high, and his best buddy Barry rescued him. Wearily, Harry had to take a bus to the Q train to get to work, about an hour and a half commute each way. As a result, Harry left for work early and wasn't there to watch Richard eat his oatmeal with Bosco-flavored chocolate milk while, starting in January 1953, Iris "handled" baby Jamie. Daily life brought Richard, Jamie, and Iris to the boardwalk where this must have frightened all of them.

A car was up on the boardwalk—it was pretty wide—and I was halfway down a boardwalk ramp when he turned to come down the ramp and the driver claimed that the sun was in his eyes so he didn't see me. His car knocked me over and rolled over my leg, which was submerged into the sand, and didn't take the full weight of the car. But I remember my mother screamed and a policeman who was nearby blew his whistle and the driver stopped before the rest of the car ran me over with the rear wheel. I remember the policeman picking me up—don't remember whose car took me to the doctor who then put iodine yellow liquid on my leg that stung me very badly. I remember being home in bed for a while after that, not sure how long. And I remember having to pee into a milk bottle and otherwise hopping to the bathroom to keep the weight off my leg. I was probably not much older than three—long before kindergarten.

—Richard

First tar pits then a car? Maybe this was an impetus to escape to the safer suburbs. The neighborhood kids played stickball and the usual street games. There were always risks.

There were six couples who became lifelong friends and continued to socialize until they moved apart or passed away. The Greissmans, Bledsoes, Perlmutters, Ostovers, Shatzs, and Lafers would all meet as the "East Thirty-Sixth Street Crowd" and go to each other's family functions. Maybe it was because they were Brooklynites, but Jamie recalls that "they were SOOOOO loud" and funny. Meetings would be filled with laughter.

Much time was spent in each other's homes. Brooklyn ties were hard to deny. There were trips to visit Aunt Anna, and to Harry's mother Mary. Grandpa Aaron lost a leg and died from diabetic complications before Jamie could even remember him, but she recalls watching a portly but frail woman, mostly deaf and blind, work feverishly on her old foot-powered Singer sewing machine. Jamie says her sewing resulted from those times. Richard recalls that in order to see Mary had to use a very thick plate of glass that was even thicker than the bottom of a Coke bottle—about 8 × 10 on a metal stand.

I remembered looking at her through that glass and yelling into her hearing horn to say hello, but there wasn't much interaction. Looking at her through her glasses magnified her eyes so much she looked like Gollum from Lord of the Rings.

For her to hear, they had to yell into her pipe shaped hearing aid. The kids never knew why.

Ehhh? What?

Richard, being two years older, has vague memories of Uncle Abe, the recluse postal worker who never married. But he owned lots of cool things that Harry's brood didn't have until much later. He had a really cool convertible, and an entertainment center with a stereo system long before they did. They inherited Abe's stereo.

Eldest brother Jacob and his wife lived in an apartment building on Riverside Drive, in Manhattan. Jacob was an engineer who invented the pneumatic road tube counter that counted traffic flow. Today you still see the hoses that cross the road. No, they aren't speed traps as I once thought.

Harry's sister, Dorothy, lived farther away, near Uncle Sol, in Scranton, Pennsylvania. The family would occasionally go on long trips to visit her and her son Robert who was near Richard's age. Sol was a happy-go-lucky, carefree guy who was youthful and dashing in his own way. They all heard stories from the wives (Anita and Iris) about putting up with Saul's partying ways—sleeping in the bathtub or what we would of called crashing at their homes. He resembled Harry, especially in his tennis outfit with the same bony legs. He always had a camera. He was a professional photographer who nurtured Richard's interest in photography that lasts until today.

Harry was an avid follower of the Dodgers and Jackie Robinson. Oddly, we didn't find Dodger tickets among Harry's memorabilia. How much did he pay attention to the current events of the era or did he, like most during the 1950s, ignore the great issues of the day and retreated into their personal lives?

Twentieth-century family photo albums document the lives of children as Instagram and I-photo do now. The same was true of the Greissmans. Living in the 1950s and 1960s meant having the newest consumer cameras. So, one of the first pictures of Richard was taken with the newest of the new, a Polaroid "instant" camera. Before digital and cellphone cameras, all pictures were on film that had to be developed by firms like Kodak. The process took days until Edwin Hand developed his Polaroid Land Camera that would produce an instant picture that developed in front of your eyes in about sixty seconds like the photo of Harry, Iris, and baby Richard that bragged it was "finished in just sixty seconds." Harry had a knack of writing captions like "Guess who was given whom a bath?" Note the correct usage of *who* and *whom*.

http://www.edn.com/electronics-blogs/edn-moments/4407362/
Polaroid-introduces-the-instant-camera--February-21--1947

Playing outside was common as well, even for toddlers.

A FIFTIES FAMILY

Fifties parents stressed the importance of the attachment to home, family, and children. They were children of the Depression. Many had seen their fathers lose their jobs and their families struggle to make ends meet. They viewed strong families as especially desirable because hard times had weakened so many families. Then came World War II and Korea, which disrupted families again and again. At last the long postwar 1950s peacetime economic boom changed their luck and gave them the prosperity to satisfy their desire for stability at work and at home. Harry dared not sacrifice the security of his job to be a writer of more than ad copy. Iris stayed home and for a while was the typical housewife, running the household and raising a family.

Much of 1950s life was either shaped or depicted by the newest must-have gadget in everyone's home, the TV. Television both reflected and altered American lives. The early 1950s birthed TV as we know it. Maybe TV also birthed the 1950s.

Perhaps the most significant shows were the situation comedies. These thirty-minute shows helped people laugh at their fictional (or not) selves. Whether imitating reality or creating real imitators, they were extremely popular and could be watched by the whole family. Some were more antic based, like *I Love Lucy* starring Lucille Ball or *The Honeymooners* starring Jackie Gleason. But many pictured the new American dream home in the suburbs, albeit with a few wrinkles.

Did *Father Know Best*? Why would anyone *Leave It to Beaver*? *The Adventures of Ozzie and Harriet* gave you a sanitized peek at the Nelson family, semi-celebrities whose sons, David and especially Ricky, gained fame as actors and rock and roll crooners. *The Danny Thomas Show* and *The Donna Reed Show* as well as others created an idyllic view of what American life should be, although that was tough to accomplish for most Americans.

> *Television's idea of a perfect family was a briefcase-toting professional father who left daily for work, and a pearls-wearing, nurturing housewife who raised their mischievous boys and obedient girls.*[72]

The Greissmans were that family. Harry was the briefcase-toting, fedora-wearing, and pipe-smoking commuting father. Iris was, while in Brooklyn until 1957, that pearl- (probably costume) wearing housewife and nurturing mother. Richard was clearly the fairly obedient son, easily attacked by tar pits and cars, and Jamie, born almost two years after Richard, on January 27, 1953, was the mischievous younger daughter. There were, however, subtle differences. Iris went off to work about the time Jamie went to kindergarten and worked throughout their suburban lives. That was very different from most middle-class white suburban American families.

This story might have been written for any of those TV family sitcoms, yet was true.

> *When Iris was pregnant with Jamie, Harry turned to his sister-in-law Ruth and said,*
> *"I don't understand what's going on. Every time I turn around, Iris is pregnant."*
> *Ruth turned to him and replied,*
> *"That's the problem Harry. Stop turning around."*

TV also provided leisure for adults and older kids as they relaxed at home after long days of work or housekeeping watching dramas like *Gunsmoke*, *Alfred Hitchcock Presents*, and *Dragnet*. Former radio stars like Jack Benny, Red Skelton, and Burns and Allen converted their comedy shows to TV. A show that would now be considered too racist for TV, *Amos 'n' Andy* was a hit. Radio and movie comedy stars like Groucho Marx took advantage of the new medium through his game show, *You Bet your Life*. Celebrity fests, *I've Got a Secret* and *What's My Line?* were other big game shows. Variety shows like *Your Show of Shows* and *The Ed Sullivan Show* entertained and thrilled families all over the country. Families enjoyed wholesome adventure series like *The Adventures of Superman*.

The effect of this infusion of TV into so many lives so often was a greater homogenization of American society. How different that process is from what the Internet and social media is doing to polarize American society today. Of course, all of those shows were saturated by the ads of the day, some of them by Harry.

Harry worked hard and long even when the kids were young. Richard, Jamie, and later Allan remember that he was rarely home early. In fact, he was more often late. Richard's earliest memories of his dad were in his tennis outfits—with shorts, a growing belly, a sweater, and really skinny legs. But there were times when Harry had really devoted himself to Richard.

Saturday morning cartoons or children's shows became the new babysitters, forever influencing the baby boomer generation. *Howdy Doody*, *Romper Room*, *Captain Kangaroo*, *Kukla, Fran, and Ollie*, *Andy Panda*, and *Bozo the Clown* fascinated kids as they learned through the characters' antics.

Harry took Richard to the circus and to a local amusement park in Rye, New York, where the two of them went on a mini roller coaster called the "Wild Mouse." Scared as he was and clinging to the bar, Richard looked over at his dad and they were laughing together. Together they strolled through the park, holding hands while Richard would look up and see Harry's sweet smile. Yet, as was the manly style of those from Harry's generation, there was not much hugging.

What father would take his young three-year-old son to *Howdy Doody* actually dressed as Howdy Doody and sit in the Peanut Gallery with the other kids and their parents? Harry did and apparently enjoyed it. Too bad we don't have any visual evidence of that.

But we have visual evidence of what Richard looked like.

Harry also took Richard into Manhattan to go the Museum of Natural History and the Hayden Planetarium. Looking up at the manufactured night sky awed them both. They felt lost in the universe because the room was so big. Richard had brought a camera with him and was so awestruck he left it behind. When they went back to get it, Harry seemed more bemused than angry. But that seemed to be the Harry way. When Richard would, as he often did, pick something up off the floor and try to chew it, Harry, who looked so big to a small child, simply took it away and told him not to. No anger. No punishments. No yelling.

When the family moved to Ardsley, Iris became a suburban oddity, a working mom. Although TV scenes usually depicted the suburban American family eating breakfast and dinner together, that was not the case in many American families, or the Greissman household. Harry was off to work before the kids had breakfast. Iris would be sure the children and she all ate dinner together early enough for them to do homework and left a plate for Harry to eat when he returned home. Sometimes she sat with him, but most times he ate alone, catching up in the newspaper, with a Dewars on the rocks. Those scenes were definitely not part of sitcom America.

They did become more commonplace a generation later. Starting in the late 1960s and 1970s more and more women went to work for one or both of these two reasons: More and more families needed two incomes to be able to have the same purchasing power and the women's movement liberated many women from the doldrums of housekeeping lives.

TICKY TACKY HOUSES
ALL IN A ROW

What Harry's family did share of the 1950s middle-class aspiration was the American dream of home ownership. The American dream became a reality when the move from the city to the suburbs became prominent in the 1950s. The stereotypical home, with the matching car and perfect family, became the new American life.

> *This is the new suburbia, the packaged villages that have become the dormitory of the new generation of organization men. They are not typical American communities, but because they provide such a cross section of young organization people we can see in bolder relief than elsewhere the kind of world organization man wants and may in time bring about.*[73]

In 1956 Ruth and Joe, himself a briefcase-toting lawyer, moved to Woodmere, Long Island. Why? Besides the trend to move to the new suburbs, houses on their Borough Park block became "shuls" (synagogues). The neighborhood started to become what it still is today, home to the largest Orthodox population outside of Israel. There was a big Jewish temple on the corner, and two doors down, a Jewish school. PS 103, their local public school closed because all the children went to Jewish schools. The Orthodox wouldn't associate with others unless "the others" followed their ways. So, either you joined or you left.

Orthodox Jews are strict followers of the Old Testament. Many men are easily recognizable in their centuries-old traditional black-and-white European garb, black hats, beards, and long "payes" (what the long, curly, not quite sideburns, hairy "corners" of one's head are called). They believe that the written and oral Torah is the exact and divine words of God. Although only 10 percent of American Jews, they tend to create very large and closed-off communities, often frustrating neighboring non-Jews and Jews alike. As a result, many "others" moved away allowing the community to grow even larger. There are parallels in every major religion.

103

Much of Harry's family had already moved to Pennsylvania. Ruth and Joe Gould's family had moved to Long Island. Harry was still commuting an hour and half each way from the distant section of Brooklyn in which they lived. The American dream beckoned. Beckoning also were the close-by northern suburbs in Westchester County with the easier commute to Grand Central Station.

So, in 1957, they moved to Ardsley, New York, a "short" commuter train ride away. Twenty-two miles from midtown, Ardsley was a one-square-mile sleepy little village until three events allowed it to become a suburban haven. First was the sale of the Huntley Estate to developers who started selling reasonably priced typical small suburban ranch and split-level houses along Heatherdell Road in 1951, close to two commuter train lines into the city.

Second, in 1953, all Ardsley children were no longer schooled in one building with the completion of the Concord Road Elementary School, near where Alexander Hamilton was reported to have an artillery camp during the Battle of White Plains. When the Greissmans moved in 1957, work was well on its way to the completion of a new junior-senior high school on the 356-acre Adolph Lewisohn estate that would be within walking distance from the new house.

The third was the opening of the New York State Thruway in 1955 with exit #7 in Ardsley.[74]

Ten Kenneth Road cost Harry and Iris the ungodly sum of $17,000 in 1957, approximately $145,000 in 2016 dollars. It was a huge investment for the family. We sold it in September 2016 for $769,000. The Greissmans traveled up to "the country" to see the house while it was being built. They were one of the first families to move in. Luckily for 6-year old Richard and 4-year old Jamie, there were to be many children with whom to grow up and become longtime friends. Richard became best friends, and still is, with Bobby Alter who lived right next door. He and Jamie would go there to play while Iris and Harry went to the construction site just a few feet away. The house sat in the middle of a steep slope, rendering the back and front yards relatively unplayable for the kids. It was the only house in the development with the garage in the back, producing a large asphalt "playground" and a terraced backyard. Back then there were no mandatory railings for decks. The kids would play up there and in the warmer weather play tetherball with nothing to prevent a fall to the hard surface below. Imagine that now?

It was a very typical new 1950s suburban development filled with young families who established the neighborhood together and grew as friends as a result, so it became easy to meet many couples through their kids meeting other kids on the streets.

These peers shared the same sets of 1950s norms and values. Harry became a suburban commuter. He met Marty Conrad, a neighbor up the street, and together they would go to the train station. When Harry became best friends with fellow tennis player Marty, Jamie became lifelong friends with their daughter Donna. Either Iris or Marty would drive to the station fairly early. No one allowed Harry to drive. Harry and Marty loved playing cards—they had a bridge game with some fellow daily travelers. The train had benches that

Harry with Richard, Jamie, and Bobby Alter in the striped shirt. Jamie
with Bobby's little brother, Rich.

could be shifted so you could have two adjoining seats facing each other and they'd play
four-handed bridge.

The doors at 10 Kenneth were never locked. Richard and Jamie came home from
school and did their homework. Richard played with Bobby Alter from next door. Jamie
put on a bathrobe and called Iris at work to see what chores needed to be done. Okay, that
was a bit strange ...

Another 1950s norm existed. Although it was an all-white neighborhood, the parents
tended to stick together with their own creed, while the kids made friends with everyone,
regardless of religion. Harry and Iris's new friends were almost all Jewish, belonged to the
same B'nai B'rith group, and went to the same Temple Beth Abraham in nearby Tarrytown.
It too was housed in a brand-new facility, opened in 1956. The kids' friends were just as
likely to have names like Callahan or Scaporrelli. That eventually led to an issue when Richard married outside the faith. There was one black family, the father was an NFL executive.

Similarly, to the East Thirty-Sixth Street Crowd, there was a Kenneth Road network
regardless of whether or not the kids were friends. The Greissmans, Fagins, Kagels, Charn-
ins, Rosens, Nassaus, and Friedmans shared long-lasting bonds even when they moved, as
became the custom, to Florida later in life. When the Friedman's son Randy fell to his death
from Yosemite Falls on a teen tour, the families pulled even closer. Tennis was a constant
with Edgar Finsmith, who lived two doors down.

An added bonus of moving to Ardsley is that it put Harry nearer to the brother he would spend the most time with. Lou and his wife, Anita, lived in upper Westchester County, along Lake Mahopac where Harry, Iris, and the kids would often go. Their daughter, Susan, was one year younger than Richard, and one year older than Jamie, so they took turns playing together.

Louis was fairly affluent. His house was very modern, with a very manicured lawn and gardens, a large backyard, and a dock with a boat on the lake. They had a garage with two cars. Lou was very fond of Cadillacs and always had at least one.

Visits there were always difficult because it was clear that Harry and Iris did not like Anita. It was especially hard on Iris because Anita was cold and often condescending. Iris would talk about how uncomfortable she was around her. Anita could be harsh and opinionated. She was somewhat cold and austere. This was unfortunate, because Lou was Harry's closest relative, both emotionally and geographically. Regardless, Lou and Harry were inseparable. The speedboat was a great attraction for the kids that always gave young Richard a thrill to ride and even drive the boat. Harry was not much of a water person. He didn't water ski, but the kids did. Iris would get in the water to wade but was not a swimmer. There was a lovely, well-positioned, slate deck where the parents could sit, play cards together, yet watch the kids playing in the water.

Susan …

Now really doesn't this look like an average ranch house? Uncle Harry would describe this house as a mansion on the lake. You would have thought we were part of the Hearst fortune. I think it was important for my Dad and Harry to feel successful and I think Mahopac was symbolic.

She recalls,

Harry was always my father's favorite. He was so proud of his kid brother. I know that Harry was very proud of his big brother too. I'm not sure of it but it seems so.

The house at 274 East Lake Drive in 2017.

I think Harry was very real with my father. I remember them sitting in our dining room at Lake Mahopac drinking scotch at my father's little table overlooking the lake and talking for hours. It wasn't a conversation I was involved in but you could tell they were really talking to each other.

When Lou had a stroke and lost his speech, Harry was devastated. He shared Lou's frustration when he struggled with words and slurred his speech. Harry was the very attentive, caring brother who saw a lot of Lou during that time, visiting him in the hospital and later when he was recovering. It must have been a crushing blow to have his closest and most worshipped sibling so debilitated.

There is a stereotype about Jewish men. Okay, there are many, but this one is important in understanding Harry as a suburban house owner. Jewish men don't use tools. They hire the men who use tools. Harry tried to break that stereotype, although usually unsuccessfully. He bought all the tools. I mean every single one of them. Some of them have outlasted him by twenty years. He even built a workbench in the back of the garage. He made shelves to store items, yet his insecurity about his ability led him to use fifteen over-sized nails when two thinner ones would suffice. There was no such thing as a joint when it was easier to nail two pieces of wood together. Somehow the ugly bench and shelves never fell apart. You have to give him credit. His talents were tennis and writing, not cabinetry.

However, when Richard was in the Cub Scouts it became time to do the "soap box" derby. During the 1950s building and racing these non-motorized boxcars on roller skates became a suburban rage. Richard had to make his own racecar out of a soft block of wood. Harry used his "skills" to help Richard make the car.

Left: A wished for soapbox derby car. Right: What Harry and Richard's more likely looked like.

Let's just say it made it down the track.

Harry did, however, somehow hone a particular "hands on" skill. Back in the days of wooden tennis rackets Harry strung his own racquet with an awl, and what Richard describes as a "round piece of wood, magically getting the tension right without a gauge or warping the racquet." I understood that when I saw Harry do that with my own eyes. I played baseball as a kid with wooden bats that sometimes used to crack at the handle and balls that would get the skins scuffed and torn from being used on asphalt or concrete.

This early 1970s picture shows Ardsley in all its glory, virtually unchanged
from when they moved in.
http://www.ardsleyvillage.com/home/slideshows/
ardsley-historical-photo-gallery

My Depression dad taught me how to fix the bats with small nails while electric tape
was used to resurface the balls as he had.

Being in the suburbs now called for a lot more driving than Harry had done while in
Brooklyn. Iris would drive the family places, not him. He was a terrible driver. Sometimes
though, he would take the car to tennis or to "downtown" Ardsley and get lost for hours.

The family never knew if he was lost, had an accident, or two, stopped to chat for
hours, or was sneaking a smoke.

Just as in those TV sitcoms, Ten Kenneth became a place for friends and family. Harry
and Iris, mostly Iris, would entertain in their small dining room. The kids, as kids then and
now did, retreated to their rooms, once permitted, to play with each other or with friends.
Ruth's children, cousins Arnie and June, were so much older that they babysat until Richard
and Jamie went to bed and then went back with the adults.

Harry and Iris's social life revolved around card playing. Iris loved to cook and entertain, Harry was charming but could be an inconsistent conversationalist in social situ-
ations. There were some dinner parties with long silences because he didn't participate a
great deal, yet there were others where he would dominate the conversations.

The East Thirty-Sixth Street Crowd visited each other on a rotating basis. Work
friends would sometimes, but less often, come around. Paul Zangas, the creative art director at Richardson-Merrell, was Harry's closest work friend with whom Harry played tennis
together and sometimes went out.

Harry would, on occasion, invite other work friends like Ben McClure, a "big boss"
vice president, a very cosmopolitan guy, who had lived in France. Ben and Harry sometimes went out with the wives but their friendship was out of sight in the workplace. Was
it because Harry was an underling or Jewish? We don't know. It was another 1950s thing.

A Mensch
Among Mad Men

Everyone (okay, maybe not everybody) knows Don Draper, Pete Campbell, and Roger Sterling of *Mad Men* fame. They represent many of the ad men of the 1950s through 1970s. *Rolling Stone* described them in a May 11, 2015, article by Rob Sheffield as "depraved rogues … with so few moral standards."[75]

Harry never saw the show. I assume he would have silently thought as George Lois, a huge Madison Avenue figure thought,

> *The more I think and write about Mad Men, the more I take the show as a personal insult. So fuck you, Mad Men, you phony grey-flannel-suit, male-chauvinist, no-talent, Wasp, white-shirted, racist, anti-Semitic Republican SOBs!*
>
> *George's and [probably Harry's] issue with Mad Men was, I think, that it was all too real—and it reminded them of everything they hated about the business as they had found it.*[76]

George felt insulted, but in fact it was all too real.

Alen Sands York and Sandy Teller were real 1960s ad men who were depicted on the hit TV show *Mad Men*. Here is their take.

The cigarette haze? True. The three-martini buzz? True. The interoffice intrigue? True. Alen York ran a Manhattan ad agency through much of the decade. He remembered,

> *Impeccably dressed, impressively paid, mostly white men convinced a nation to buy whatever they were selling. And yes, the ad agency ethos included plenty of nicotine, booze and dips in the steno pool. It was the Wild West. Yes, there were beautiful women around. And there was a certain glamour from the outside to the industry— maybe more than it deserved.*

109

Rose Mendicino, a secretary at Ketchum, MacLeod & Grove, is convinced some of the *"Mad Men plots came directly from the agency's creative department. Big, tall,* [Harry was 5'6"] *suited, good-looking—well, some were good looking. Definitely predators. Married or not."*

She says the women in the agency generally knew—and readily accepted—their sub-servient status. *"All the account executives, all the art directors, all the copywriters—no matter how dumb—were men,"* she recalls. *"I don't even know if the women even thought about it that much. A lot of them were looking for husbands."*

A 1967 survey of Ketchum employees reported: Three-quarters of the secretaries polled said they would marry an ad man if given the chance.

Sandy Teller, head of Sanford Teller Communications, remembers the broader, racier picture. *"There was a great sense of power and prestige."* Teller says the attitude was one of, *"I'm an advertising executive. And you're (long, disdainful pause) ... an accountant?"*

Drinking was a way of life, in and out of the office. York remembers that any impor-tant business was handled before lunch. "We always knew that after lunch, you may as well forget about doing anything," he says. "Clients, customers, three-martini lunches. They were finished for the afternoon." Standing tall at the bar was part of the macho culture that dominated the industry. "In many cases, there was great admiration for the guys who could drink more, as if it was a great skill or talent."

There was also the rush of whipping up an ad campaign overnight, without the "ben-efit" of focus groups or demographics snapshots—just your gut, a pack of Lucky Strikes, and a long lunch. Says York,

> *It was seat of the pants, and it was fun. I'd do it again if I had the chance.*[77]

Little of that sounds like the Harry Greissman his family knew and loved. However, as a man of the times he had to go along to get along. He loved his work, and maybe those "three martini lunches" witnessed by his oldest son Richard, but it is hard to believe he was like those Mad Men. Perhaps he played along to fit in, or perhaps Harry had a totally different persona at work than at home. Or perhaps being Jewish left him on the outside looking in. After all, his friendship with Ben McClure was out of work sight.

His daughter Jamie recalls sometimes going to work with Harry when she didn't have school.

While there, she didn't see Mad Men. To her Harry was very proud to both show them (including brother Richard) off to his coworkers and show off his work to them. She would clean up his usually messy desk and dine at the "luxurious" Horn & Hardart. Horn & Hardart was a twentieth-century marvel. None of this sounds very *Mad Men*–like.

> *A coin-operated glass-and-chrome wonder, Horn & Hardart's Automats revolutionized the way Americans ate when they opened up in Philadelphia and New York in the early twentieth century. In a country where the industrial revolution had just taken hold, eating at a restaurant with self-serving vending machines rather than waitresses and Art Deco architecture instead of stuffy dining rooms was an unforgettable experience.*

The Automat served freshly made food for the price of a few coins, and no one made a better cup of coffee. By the peak of its popularity—from the Great Depression to the post-war years—the Automat was more than an inexpensive place to buy a good meal; it was a culinary treasure, a technical marvel, and an emblem of the times.[78]

Richard would go to Harry's office on school holidays. After Harry would very proudly introduce him to everybody in the office, Richard would go to the art department where he would visit with Harry's best friend, art director, Paul Zangas. Paul would give Richard colored pencils and paper and when older, let him use an intriguing wonderful machine: a light table and magnifier that would allow the user to sketch a larger version of a design. Richard would design cough drop boxes. He remembers Harry laughing heartily when Richard proudly displayed a design with a misspelled "cough dorps."

> *I came in when someone was with him, the friend noticed it and they both laughed and I was embarrassed.*

Harry first worked at Morse International when it became the in-house advertising agency for Vick International, located in the Chanin Building, 122 East 42nd Street, Manhattan, New York. Every day he walked through this magnificent entry.

Jamie recalls, "He used to love to get his shoes shined in the lobby of the Chanin building. It seemed so luxurious. I remember watching as a little girl and being entertained by the shoe shiner; always a Black man who would entertain, use humor, and would whistle or sing songs."

The building still is a marvel of Art Deco design filled with beautiful interior marble and metal works. It's location, directly across the street from Grand Central Station, was why Harry broke ranks with most Brooklynites who moved to the Long Island suburbs. The Metro North trains (then called the New York Central) terminated in Grand Central. The Long Island Rail Road trains terminated in Pennsylvania Station, over a mile and close

to 20 minutes farther west at 8th Avenue and 33rd Street. Harry chose instead to conveniently take the Harlem line from Hartsdale to Grand Central daily until the early 1980s when his company moved to Wilton, Connecticut.

Richard recalls commuting with Harry.

When you got near Grand Central Station and the lights in the train would always go off for a period of time while the train was still moving so you'd be in the dark with only an occasional construction light. It always seemed like the longest time though it was probably only a few minutes. We'd gather up our things and everyone was always in a rush—we'd have to walk real fast. We went upstairs through a revolving door into the next building. I remember walking through the main lobby of the Station and being so amazed at how big it was, and the clock, the hustle-and-bustle.

The conductors in their hats hand-punch a hole in our ticket. We'd always try to get the Express train, but I remember being on the train when the conductor would announce many more stops than were typical when you had the Express. I remember the revolving door because one time I was a little sluggish getting into the door and I lost my shoe—I had to wait until someone retrieved my shoe.

The Morse agency was one of the oldest ad agencies in the country, becoming Morse International in 1906. During the 1950s Morse became the in-house ad agency for Vick International Chemical Company started by Lundsford Richardson in 1905 to market various home remedies, including what would become the world famous Vicks VapoRub.

By the time Harry was working there, it was marketing other cold remedy products such as nose sprays, cough drops, prescription drugs, and toiletries. The company name was changed to Richardson-Merrell in 1960 and to Richardson-Vicks in 1981. Its health care and consumer brands included Lavoris, Cepacol, Clearasil, Nyquil, and Oil of Olay, which Richardson-Vick purchased in 1970.

http://ncpedia.org/biography/
richardson-lunsford

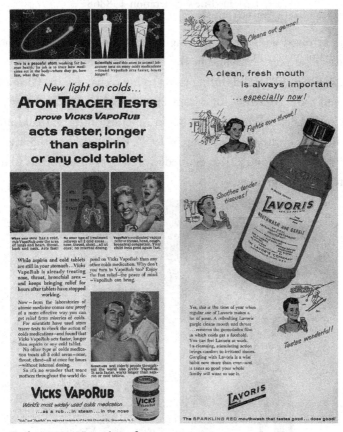

Early 1950s: Note the reference to atomic power.
http://ncpedia.org/biography/richardson-lunsford 1957:
http://library.duke.edu/digitalcollections/mma_MM0332/

1970.
http://www.adweek.com/news/advertising-
branding/how-postwar-beauty-cream-oil-
olay-freshened-new-generation-158868

Harry was involved with the advertising for each, and made sure his household had plenty. For thirty-nine years everyone in the family had a lifetime supply of VapoRub, Lavoris, Cepacol, Oil of Olay, and during those trying teenage years, Clearasil.[79]

Unfortunately, the company for whom Harry would work for forty years was also involved in the most horrible consumer issues in American history: thalidomide.

Thalidomide was created in Germany in 1957. By 1960, the drug was in more than twenty countries in Europe and Africa as a sedative to treat insomnia as well as to reduce nausea associated with pregnancy.

http://guides.main.library.emory.edu/c.
php?g=50422&p=325039

> *On Sept. 12, 1960, Richardson-Merrell Inc. submitted a New Drug Application to market thalidomide in the U.S. under the brand name Kevadon. Dr. Frances O. Kelsey was assigned to review this request by the Food and Drug administration was troubled by the lack of evidence that the drug was safe for human use. Her insistence on sufficient documentation kept thalidomide off the U.S. market for over a year, sufficient time for doctors to uncover the link between thalidomide and birth defects.*

Although thalidomide was never licensed in the United States, it was distributed as samples to American doctors to try with their patients. It was common practice at that time for drug companies to pass on experimental drugs to doctors, who were then paid to collect data on their patients' results. Patients did not normally know or consent to their part in this loosely controlled research. In 1962, the drug was taken off the market, but not before 10,000 children had been impacted. It is estimated that 40 percent of babies with thalidomide-induced birth defects died before their first birthday.[80]

Harry clearly was a company man. After all, he worked at the same place for almost forty years. Once at the dinner table, Richard said,

> *Look at what happened when a drug company manufactured a drug to help women to deal with pregnancy issues—Thalidomide—and how horrific that was.*

Harry threw down his napkin and said that was his company. Upset and angry, he left the table. Richard thinks Harry was angry with him for speaking out against the company although he had presented it as an issue of malfeasance by a company that was suppressing known problems they had been researching for years, "and yet I think he was angry with me because I was sounding anti-corporate."

That was a generational norm. Harry stayed with that company for his entire career. The men of his Greatest Generation, probably more than my boomer generation, and definitely more than the subsequent generations, X and millennial, were career men. They often worked for the same company for decades and then received their gold watch or golf clubs when they left decades later.

It seems he followed the David Ogilvy occupational mobility mantra as depicted in his famous 1963 book, *Confessions of an Advertising Man*. Whether Ogilvy knew it or not, what he described was not just fitting for his industry, his descriptions of the maturation of "Every Industry Man" was almost universal in how it fit men of Harry's generation.

Ogilvy stressed youth in the "creatives" of his industry and that after a while they run out of ideas and no longer do well for the company. He simply noted that if they were good loyal employees they would get kicked upstairs as did so many men of that generation. That was Harry.

If not, or if they were more ambitious, they would look for work elsewhere. According to Ogilvy, an executive responsible for keeping clients had to be stable and easy to get along with. That also was Harry.

Harry went from being a creative (the ad maker), to a creative director (the boss of the ad makers) to an international marketing executive (the seller of ads internationally).

His company, whatever name it had, (Morse, Vick International, Richardson-Merrell, Richardson Vicks) at the time kept him on for thirty-nine years. Harry was good, loyal, and in search more for security than ambitious job changes. He was, after all, that universal Depression child of the Greatest Generation for whom security and safety were mantras.

Harry did rise through the ranks. In time, as a result of his fluency in so many languages, he became important to a company who did so much increasing business overseas. In the 1950s US companies extended operations into Latin America. Vicks opened a plant in Mexico. They sold heavily in many Latin countries such as Venezuela where 40 percent of imported consumer goods came from the United States.

We know Procter & Gamble eventually purchased Richardson-Vicks in 1985 because they wanted to grow their overseas markets in Japan and Latin America. Vicks products were a huge part of that expansion. Harry became their lead man there.

The 1950s and early 1960s were the eras of military juntas controlling Latin American countries and "Ugly American" corporations taking advantage of Latin nations. It led to the growth of rebel groups and resulted in Vice President Richard Nixon being attacked with stones when he visited Venezuela in May 1958. Was Harry in danger as well?

He still had that Pan Am bag when he died.

THE TIMES, THEY ARE A CHANGIN'

Harry kept two now very yellowed *New York Times* copies, each with big bold headlines.

KENNEDY'S VICTORY WON BY CLOSE MARGIN; HE PROMISES FIGHT FOR WORLD FREEDOM

NIXON RESIGNS HE URGES A TIME OF 'HEALING'

These two headlines effectively mark the beginning and the end of one of the most intriguing eras in our history. Commonly called the 60s, the era actually spans from the Kennedy administration to the downfall of Richard Nixon fourteen years later. Political, economic, and social changes effectively turned the nation into camps, some armed. The worsening of the Cold War, the Civil Rights Movement, the Women's Movement, the War in Vietnam, and the many cultural changes in American culture brought on by a new music rocked us to the core. It turned normal gaps between the generations into "the generation gap."

Harry and Iris, like the rest of their generation, grew up during the Great Depression and became adults during World War II and the early 1950s. They desperately tried to normalize lives that were severely disrupted by the most devastating decades of the century. Finally, as a married couple, they raised their children in a manner reflecting the American dream they hoped to live. They secured a safe home for them. They made sure they had a good education and provided for their future. Like so many others of their generation, they wanted nothing more than upward mobility for their children.

However, because of the drastically changing times, a growing fear of total nuclear destruction by Cold War rivals, riots in the streets, and the potential of a soldier's death, they also prayed for the safety of their children. We had been a peacetime nation since 1953. Of course, there were a few "little issues" that popped up from time to time, but the biggest threat was nuclear annihilation. This threat had grown since the 1950s with the advent of far superior means of dropping atomic bombs.

The Cold War was more than a war of words. It was a race to develop the most destructive weapons known to mankind and the fastest ways to get them to their targets. In 1950, the United States had 299 nuclear bombs deliverable by our long-range bombers. No one else but the Soviets had any, and they had only five. We were not worried. In 1955, we had 2,422. Who knows why? Not I. The Russians, however, had 200 and now had an air force more capable of delivering them to targets within the United States. That scared us.

Each side worked to improve the "delivery system" both feared most, the rockets first developed by German scientists during World War II. In fact, after the war both countries competed to give asylum to the best of those scientists. One could accurately say that the Germans won the space race. Fear became our pastime.

At first, both the United States and Russia had air forces with some capability to do that, but the real threat didn't occur until 1957. Then came Sputnik. On October 4, 1957, a Russian missile successfully launched a basketball-sized object on a 98-minute ride around the globe.

The Sputnik launch marked the start of the space age and the US–USSR space race, which drastically changed the course of events for millions across the world. Bombs now became nuclear warheads attached to missiles like the one that lifted Sputnik into space and could be here in minutes. In 1960, we had over 18,000 warheads and the Russians had 1,600. By the time Nixon resigned from the presidency, in 1974, we had over 27,000 warheads while the Russians had almost 20,000. What the?[81]

There were enough warheads to blow the world to bits and pieces. The policy was simple. Called mutually assured destruction (MAD), both sides each built so many weapons to "assure" that neither would actually use them because it would lead to the total destruction of the planet. It was madness, and yet both fearfully and hopefully we all lived through it at the time. During the early 1960s the Cold War almost flared up into a hot war twice, and into a real proxy war once.

Stanley Kubrick's classic 1964 film, *Dr. Strangelove or: How I Learned to Stop Worrying and Love the Bomb* satirically had an insane general trigger a path to nuclear holocaust.

Public and urban apartment buildings built fully stocked bomb shelters in basements while suburban families like Harry's seriously considered building underground shelters in the backyard, especially in the fall of 1962, when during the Cuban Missile Crisis, we came the closest to nuclear war.

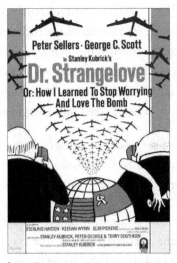

*https://www.movieposter.com/
poster/MPW-31779/Dr_Strange-
love.html*

http://www.u-s-history.com/pages/
h3706.html

People were scared. Schools developed useless duck and cover drills. We called them "Get on your knees and kiss your ass goodbye" drills. While I was teaching in a New York City high school in the 1970s, I happened to be at the front entrance to the school when a naval officer arrived. He was there to talk to seniors about a naval career.

As I walked him to the correct office four bells rang four times in rapid succession. When the officer heard those, he asked what it was. I told him it was an air raid drill. During these drills students stayed at their desks until told to form a line at the door, single file and no talking. From there, they were to go into the corridor away from windows and kneel down facing the wall with their heads down on their knees. They were to clasp their hands over the back of their necks to protect their spinal cords from flying glass. He just laughed.

I had already known it was a silly drill. If a nuke landed anywhere near us there would be no building, let alone flying glass. When I asked him what was so funny, he paused and said.

> *Look. Suppose there was a Soviet submarine twelve miles off the coast of New York that fired its load of nuclear missiles. What makes you think the first people we notify would be the NYC Board of Education?*

The big question of the era was more about what event might precipitate such an attack. Nineteen sixty-one then became a harrowing year. The events that most worried us concerned Germany and Cuba. Not only did the Soviets and East Germans erect the Berlin Wall, an American-supported invasion of the Bay of Pigs in Cuba ended in fiasco and almost led to a nuclear war. Television brought both into our living rooms.

Following World War II, Germany and its capital, Berlin, had been divided into East and West sections. The Soviets controlled both East Germany and East Berlin. Since the end of World War II the Soviets continuously tried to push the western powers out of West Berlin, which was deep inside East Germany. Following John F. Kennedy's inauguration in January 1961, the Soviets and the puppet East German state again wanted to close off the passageways from East to West Berlin, as many Easterners fled west.

Six months after his inauguration, President John F. Kennedy gave a speech before the border between East and West Berlin was to be closed.

> *Those who threaten to unleash the forces of war on a dispute over West Berlin should recall the words of the ancient philosopher: "A man who causes fear cannot be free from fear."*[82]

Soviet Premier Nikita Khrushchev responded:

> *You convinced yourself that Khrushchev will never go to war ... so you scare us [expecting] us to retreat. True, we will not declare war, but we will not withdraw either ...*[83]

Two weeks later construction of the infamous Berlin Wall began. Nerves frayed. The tension increased. Two years later Kennedy went to West Berlin and gave his famous "Ich bin ein Berliner" ("I am a Berliner.") speech.

Meanwhile, back in the western hemisphere, Fidel Castro, a self-proclaimed democratic rebel leader, took control of Cuba in January 1959. A year later he established a relationship with the Soviet Union and took over US oil refineries in Cuba. Faced with a communist dictatorship, many Cubans left to America, a mere ninety miles away, in droves. Others were actually kicked out of their own homeland. This led President Kennedy to authorize the unfortunate Bay of Pigs invasion by Cuban exiles in 1961.

Although the invasion was conceived during the Eisenhower administration, Kennedy reluctantly approved its action but denied air support in the hopes of concealing a US role in the effort. In April 1961, approximately 1,300 Cuban exiles armed with US weapons landed at Bahia de Cochinos (the Bay of Pigs) on the southern coast of Cuba. They hoped to gain support from the local population, cross the island to Havana, and overthrow Castro. However, Castro's army quickly defeated them. It was a fiasco for the first-year president and led the Russians to think Kennedy was a rank amateur.

The next month Castro solidified his ties with the Soviets, declared himself a Marxist-Leninist (Communist), and accepted increased economic and military aid from the Soviets. Our response was to declare a full economic embargo that President Obama finally started to reverse last year. American families', like Harry's, fears grew as they followed these alarming stories.

Khrushchev's underestimation of President Kennedy led to an unfortunate decision. He and Castro agreed to secretly place nuclear missiles in Cuba, a mere ninety miles from the shores of Florida. Duh, secrets don't last long, especially with invisible spy planes taking very clear long-range photos.

We discovered the missiles and their bases as they were being built. Kennedy responded by demanding the bases deconstructed and the missiles removed. He ordered the US Navy to stop and search any Russian ships on their way to Cuba. Each step was duly reported in print, TV, and radio news media. This was going to be the end of the world.

That was extraordinary. It had come down to a showdown, a poker game. Was the world finally reaching the point of no return? Who was bluffing? Who was going to blink first? Would the Russians turn their ships around? Would Americans board, search, and maybe seize Russian ships? Would that lead to war? Would it be nuclear? Would we all die?

For thirteen days Americans like Harry, Iris, and maybe at this point 10-year-old Richard and 8-year-old Jamie, held their breath. I was really nervous. Most Americans were. Were we ready to bend over and kiss our big American asses goodbye?

Thankfully, following secret back-channel negotiations, the Russians turned their ships around and agreed to remove the missiles and their bases in return for the US removal of similar bases in Turkey, along the Russian southern border, and an agreement not to invade Cuba. Rank amateur indeed. Almost three years to the day, Khrushchev was overthrown, mostly because of that failed understanding of Kennedy. Two years after the showdown and five months after that Berlin speech, Kennedy was assassinated.

Putin learned this behavior from somewhere. Just sayin'.

Did Father Know Best?

How much was life in the Greissman household emulating that 1950s TV sitcom sense of family? Back at 10 Kenneth, Richard and Jamie were growing up. Richard was in the Ashford Ave Middle School. Jamie's Concord Road elementary school was overflowing with new students. And now, Harry and Iris had to worry about a newborn, Allan. In 1961, after eight years of bringing up Richard and Jamie alone, accidentally, they had to start again.

Tennis was always present.

Having Allan made for an extra financial strain. Harry and Iris both worked. They both believed in their kids' futures and wanted to be sure they had enough money for two future Bar Mitzvahs, three college tuitions, and at least one wedding. Allan was toddling around. Richard and Jamie became responsible latchkey kids. Richard was becoming a well-behaved young man, and Jamie was becoming a bit "rambunctious" in school.

Sure, she was a goody-goody at home being in the Brownies and Girl Scouts, and she was already trained by Iris as a *balabusta* (a good homemaker), but in school she had a bit of difficulty with self-control. She was the mischievous one. Due to overcrowding in the K–4 elementary school a fourth grade class was made up of students who appeared older so they could more easily fit into what they called "a middle school setting" and literally moved into another building that was for fifth and sixth graders.

While there, Jerry Liu kept "taunting" her on the playground. Jamie wrote him a note saying, "You are a…. [fill in all curse words learned from older brothers]" Jerry showed the note to the teacher who told the principal, who called in Iris, who now had to take off from work. When Harry came home, he did the usual come home from work father thing.

Being stern but not harsh, he expressed his disappointment, asked her where she learned such language, and told her she should never use the words again. Father indeed knew best here.

Jamie recalls another *Father Knows Best* moment. They were at the Ardsley Swim and Tennis Club when she was around six. Harry and the family were members of this local, very inexpensive "wannabe country club." Many middle-class neighborhoods had these to fulfill the American dream of affluence in some small way. Families could have leisure at home, like the rich folk did.

The family spent many a summer there. His close tennis buddy, Edgar Finsmith, was on the board of directors. Harry wrote "copy" for the club, maybe as part of a quid pro quo to lessen the cost of belonging. Still a bit young, Jamie wanted desperately to pass the deep-water test. Wise Harry wanted her to practice in the shallow end. She started swimming but then stopped in that portion of the shallow end that was still too deep for her. He jumped in to save her in such a manner to soothe her and encourage her to try again later when she was more ready.

> *One of my fondest memories is being a little girl and him kissing me, and I would say "Daddy, you have prickers." He would laugh and love that. I loved when he recited a poem—he loved "If," "Oh Captain, My Captain," and delighted and bemoaned us with his singing rendition (he was totally tone deaf) of "Danny Boy."*

Other stories show some *Father May Not Know Best* moments that were typically Harry. Two involve driving, the other, tennis. Remember, everyone knew he was a terrible driver, with a bad sense of direction. One day Harry was alone with the kids. Driving home, in theory, from the pool and tennis club, they ended up in Scarsdale where they had an accident. Scarsdale was in the complete opposite direction from the way home, but … Harry either rammed the car in front of him or was hit from behind. Everyone assumed it was his fault. Mischievous Jamie was in shorts, but as the saying goes "commando" as her

Note the fedora in both pictures.

bathing suit was too wet to drive in. The police and an ambulance came, and they all went to the hospital. Jamie was totally embarrassed at the hospital when her "commando wear" was noticed by all. Harry had whiplash and had to wear a neck brace for weeks. Iris kept him away from the steering wheel for weeks. This was less to prevent him from getting hurt again, and more for the safety and honor of their children.

The other instance was interesting in that it revealed Harry's reluctance to do what were considered typically "manly" things. The result was a failed family trip and a huge argument. One day, they were to undertake a rare fun family day trip to Mystic, Connecticut. As Richard remembers, they didn't usually go anywhere without a specific functional purpose. Not that long after leaving the house, with Iris driving, of course, the front left tire blew while on the Connecticut Turnpike. Somehow Iris got the car over to the shoulder. Everyone was rattled. Why was Iris driving? Okay, everyone, in unison on three: Everyone was afraid of Harry's driving.

It was then custom for the man to get out of the car and fix it. With the scary "whoosh" of speeding traffic passing them, Richard, not Harry, fixed it. There were no cell phones. No one could call for a tow truck. Rather than try to make it to Mystic, they simply turned around and went home. Richard can't recall who made them go home, but he imagines it was "my dad who was concerned about how upset my mom was and that we didn't have a backup tire." I'll bet Iris was upset, not at the accident or the tire, but at Harry.

Jamie has many memories of him giving eloquent and articulate speeches, particularly with his leadership at B'nai B'rith, the temple, teaching, pitching an idea ... He mesmerized everyone with his use of language. He always somehow looked professional, whether just coming home, or deciding whether to sled with the kids or shovel their huge driveway after the blizzard of February 1961.

Harry spent much of his free time playing tennis, thereby reducing his availability to the family. Tennis was his choice, whereas many white-collared professional men of his generation had chosen golf. The resulting hours away from the family were the same.

Harry's love for tennis was both a blessing and a curse. Jamie believes, "It gave him a steady outlet, a passion for something that was extremely healthy, that was socially engaging with friends and strangers." The problem was that far more often than not it was not with the family. The kids believe that although Harry got Iris on the court at times and that she could

Tennis everywhere.   *Jamie as Peter Pan.*

have become a talented player in her own right, she rarely played because it was her way of protesting how much time it took away from her and the family. It became somewhat of an issue.

One tennis argument between Iris and Harry occurred when they were planning to visit Allan at summer camp. It was hard to know much about the accommodations near the camp, but it was a very small town. Harry obsessed over whether or not there were tennis courts nearby. He wanted to stay at a place that had tennis courts. He spent the weekend splitting time with Allan or on the courts. The weekend was supposed to be totally about Allan.

Summers for the kids meant a chance to get away from not just school but from home. Starting in 1960, Richard and Jamie went to Camp Pokono-Romona, a Jewish sleep-away camp in, or actually under, what is now the Delaware Water Gap, on the New York–Pennsylvania border. These camps had become another tradition for many middle-class families in the northeast United States. Here, kids played sports; learned about nature; did arts, crafts, and maybe drama; and developed a sense of both community and friendship.

For parents it was both a time of worry and enjoyment. They wanted to be sure their children would be safe and sound. They also got a precious eight weeks alone. So did the kids.

Parents frequently wrote letters to ensure the kids knew they weren't forgotten and still loved. The kids … not so much. Often they were forced to write back. Harry always embarrassed Jamie by addressing her letter's envelopes to: "Jamie Beth Beautiful Greissman." She now calls them "embarrassing, but good for ego development." The whole letter-writing routine became a huge source of entertainment, such as in this 1963 Grammy-winning comedy song by Allan Sherman.

Hello Muddah, hello Fadduh,
Here I am at Camp Grenada
Camp is very entertaining
And they say we'll have some fun if it stops raining.

I went hiking with Joe Spivy
He developed poison ivy
You remember Leonard Skinner
He got ptomaine poisoning last night after dinner.

All the counselors hate the waiters
And the lake has alligators
And the head coach wants no sissies
So he reads to us from something called Ulysses.

Now I don't want this should scare ya
But my bunkmate has malaria
You remember Jeffrey Hardy
They're about to organize a searching party.

Take me home, oh Muddah Fadduh, take me home, I hate Grenada
Don't leave me out in the forest where I might get eaten by a bear.
Take me home, I promise I will not make noise or mess the house with
Other boys, oh please don't make me stay, I've been here one whole day.

Dearest Fadduh, darling Muddah,
How's my precious little Bruddah?
Let me come home if ya miss me
I will even let Aunt Bertha hug and kiss me.

Wait a minute, it stopped hailing,
Guys are swimming, guys are sailing,
Playing baseball, gee that's better,
Muddah Fadduh please disregard this letter.[84]

The family, like so many others, did go on vacations to the "Jewish Alps." Either in the fall or early spring, when the rates were lower, they and Iris's family circle went to "The Homowack" or "The Granite" resorts. These were more affordable hotels that Jews could go to with that "country club air." Borscht Belt comedians and musical acts entertained the adults. Some were famous, like Buddy Hackett, Shelly Winters, Mel Brooks, or Phyllis Diller. It was Vegas east, but without the gambling. The kids swam at the indoor pool, ice-skated, and did whatever activities kids found at these places. Dirty dancing anyone?

The meals at these Jewish resorts may have been the highlight of the weekend. Stuffing oneself with food was a big part of the experience, especially because it was "all you can eat" buffet style. If you desired, you could have two or three main dishes and desserts. Maybe this was especially important for Depression kids. Maybe it was because you could eat all you wanted without paying for the extra. Maybe they were all gluttons.

Harry, in particular, loaded his plate several times. Any time Harry went to a buffet,
he ate more than most. He always had a good appetite.... but unlimited amounts of
food was a delicacy he couldn't refuse. —Jamie

Sadly, these once popular hotels were left abandoned.

The remains of the bowling alley and lobby of the Homowack.
http://www.dailymail.co.uk/travel/travel_news/article-2756693/They-ve-time-lives-Ghostly-remains-
abandoned-resorts-glitzy-Upstate-New-York-hotels-setting-Dirty-Dancing.html

Travel with Harry was troubling for everyone. He wasn't going to drive, but it seemed that anytime they were preparing to go anywhere became a "Where's Harry?" moment. We all firmly believe the makers of "Where's Waldo?" owed a debt of gratitude to Harry. Was he in the garage sneaking a smoke? Was he still in the shower? (Apparently, he would take what to others felt like month-long showers.) Was he outside chatting? It became another source of tension.

Growing up with Harry was tough for Allan, who was a "surprise". Harry was 45 when he was born, worked all day, and taught two to three nights a week. He played tennis or read the paper whenever he could. As a result, Iris primarily brought Allan up with help from Richard and Jamie. Allan recalls. "Richard was my second father just as much as an older brother."

Yet there were moments like this.

Allan on a summertime American Flyer wagon ride.

Richard, Allan, and Jamie in family portrait.

Scenes from suburbia.

Families also spent time together at holiday dinners. The Jewish New Year of Rosh Hashanah or Thanksgiving gave Iris and Ruth the chance to cook magnificent meals. Brisket, noodle pudding, cheesecake, and a Jell-O mold filled all. Harry was most remembered for the same old "Broccoli" joke, time and time again, until after a while, at the first utterance of the first easily recognizable syllable, everyone, in unison, yelled, "Harry, NOOOOOO, NOT THE BRROCCOLLIII JOKE!!!!" But, nevertheless, sometimes he couldn't help himself.

So a grocer is restocking the vegetables, when a woman taps him on the shoulder and says, "Excuse me Sir, but where do you keep the broccoli?"

The man replies, "Well ma'am we're out of broccoli today, but we will get some more tomorrow so come back then." The woman nods and walks away while the grocer continues stocking the carrots.

A few minutes later the same woman taps the grocer on the shoulder and asks, "Sir, I was wondering where I could find the broccoli?" Confused, the grocer says, "Well ma'am we are out of broccoli today. However, we will have more tomorrow morning. Come back tomorrow."

The woman smiles and thanks him as she walks away. Shaking his head, the grocer turns his attention back to the carrots. Moments later the woman again taps him on the shoulder and asks, "Pardon me, but do you know where the broccoli is?" The grocer looks at her angrily and says, "Let me ask you something. How do you spell dog, like in dogmatic?" The woman replies "D-O-G." "Okay" says the grocer. "Now how do you spell cat, as in catatonic?" "C-A-T," says the woman. "Perfect" the grocer replies.

"Now how do you spell fuck, like in broccoli?" Confused, the woman says, "But there is no fuck in broccoli." The grocer says, "THAT'S WHAT I'VE BEEN TRYING TO TELL YA LADY! THERE'S NO FUCKIN' BROCCOLI!"[85]

Harry, Ruth's son Arnie, Jamie, Ruth, Joe, Ruth's daughter June and husband Eric, Iris, and Allan in the red blazer and bow tie he made famous. Richard took the picture.

RITES OF PASSAGE

In the Jewish religion becoming Bar or Bat Mitzvah is the rite of passage for 13-year-olds to become young men or young women in the eyes of God. The more common usage of Bar or Bat Mitzvah is the ceremony and following party, but traditionally, it actually translates into "son or daughter of commandment." So, when a Jewish child becomes 13, he or she now has the same rights as a full-grown man or woman, and adult "responsibilities."

Of course, this is a bit out of touch with the modern reality. In ancient days children became adults so young because they were both almost completely socialized and usually old enough to procreate. Today, through no fault of their own, (well, maybe some) most American children can't grow up until they have reached 30, not 13.

American Bar Mitzvahs started to include fancy parties. Parties need music. One would now see how music separated the generations. The parents would dance to their old standards while the younger folk would watch, bored by it all. The kids would get to dance to their music, as the older folk would hold their hands over their ears, complain about the volume and vulgarity, or go for a drink and a smoke.

In 1964, Richard became Bar Mitzvah. Still only for boys, Jamie never became a Bat (female) Mitzvah. Bar Mitzvahs became a staple of income for the same catering halls that made their money from big weddings. Many are now as fancy as the fanciest of weddings, black tie and all. They became opportunities to compete, not with the Joneses, but with the Cohens.

Richard's was one of those catered events. There was nothing special about Richard's Bar Mitzvah. The reception was at Tappan Hill, an upscale restaurant and event center. Harry and Iris spent what was for them a small fortune. This was one of the few times Harry gladly spent money.

Harry was extremely proud of his firstborn son. When Richard finished his Torah reading and solo (the traditional reading of the Haftorah), he gave such an audible sigh of relief that everyone in the congregation heard it and laughed lovingly. At the party, Harry said a blessing over the challah, and gave a speech. He loved to do give extemporaneous,

Seated: Ruth, Harry, Iris, brother Ash's wife Marilyn.
Standing: Joe, Richard, an aunt, friends Ida and Norman Richman.

eloquent, heartfelt speeches that turned out to be quite memorable. After all, "he could make words sing."

Post–World War II America also had its own rite of passage. JFK was assassinated in 1963. The next year, 1964, Lyndon Johnson was elected president in a landslide victory over Barry Goldwater. At the time it was the most lopsided presidential victory in our history. Johnson won 486 electoral votes to Goldwater's 52. Goldwater only tallied 38 percent of the vote.

Johnson had two things going for him. First, he was basking in the glow of Kennedy's popularity. Second, Goldwater had a sad propensity for saying some really inflammatory things. He actually said he wanted to hurl a nuclear bomb into the men's room at the Kremlin. He wanted to use nuclear weapons in Vietnam where the war between North Vietnamese communists and its guerilla allies in the south and the democratic-leaning government of South Vietnam and its ally, the United States was just escalating.

http://kut.org/post/when-lbjs-infamous-daisy-ad-changed-politics-forever

The Johnson campaign brilliantly exploited American's Cold War fears with their famous "Daisy" ad. Shown only once, it featured a little girl plucking flower petals. A countdown is heard, followed by a nuclear explosion. The ad ended with a solemn narrator saying, "Vote for President Johnson on November 3. The stakes are too high for you to stay home."

All of this sounds too familiar in 2017 ... Hello, North Korea?

Little did anyone know at the time that the Vietnam War would eventually destroy Johnson and tear apart the fabric of American society. It would directly shape the nation for the rest of the 1960s and future foreign policy deep into the twenty-first century.

Nineteen sixty-four was a whirlwind year. In August 1964, Johnson asked Congress to approve the Gulf of Tonkin Resolution (the Gulf of Tonkin was where US destroyers had ALLEGEDLY been attacked by North Vietnamese patrol boats), giving him the power to use both air strikes against North Vietnam and all necessary measures to repel attacks against US forces and all steps necessary for the defense of US allies in Southeast Asia. It passed almost unanimously. We were embroiled there until 1973. It brought more fear and death to American families than they had seen since the end of World War II.

Civil rights had become a growing national battle since the mid-1950s. The Supreme Court's 1954 *Brown v. The Board of Education of Topeka, Kansas* decision ordered all US public schools to desegregate. In 1955, Rosa Parks was denied a seat on a bus in Montgomery, Alabama. Dr. Martin Luther King led protests around the nation, culminating with the famous March on Washington in 1963 when over 200,000 Americans listened to Dr. King's famous "I Have a Dream" speech, which inspired so many.

Richard was shaped by these events, even at the age of 13. But in 1964 things turned darker. Thousands of college students went south to work on voter registration drives so "negro" Americans could vote. Three of them were murdered in Mississippi. Two came from New York. One of them, Michael Schwerner, came from nearby Pelham, New York. More fear. More death. More parental worry.

On the heels of the Civil Rights Movement was the movement for the civil rights of 50 percent of the population. Nineteen sixty three brought Betty Friedan's highly influential book *The Feminine Mystique*, which told of the dissatisfaction felt by middle-class American housewives with the narrow role imposed on them by society. More women went to work, not because they had to, but because they wanted to. However, in the 1960s women like Iris were still in the minority. That year also brought the Equal Pay Act, making it illegal for employers to pay a woman less than what a man would receive for the same job. Yeah, right.

In 1964, we learned that smoking cigarettes caused cancer. American and Soviet astronauts were circling the earth. Color TV was replacing black and white. The New York World's Fair of 1964 featured high-tech demonstrations from governments and companies from around the world that would predict the future including automation and computer technology.

Even goody-goody Richard cut school to go there. All of these events contributed to the growing generation gap, but it was in music and culture where much more change was to come. Change was everywhere and the older generation couldn't keep up.

Harry and Iris enjoyed the musical standards of their day: classical music, opera, and songs by Frank Sinatra, Bing Crosby, and Tony Bennett. Even though rock and roll music had already been around for a decade, they loathed it as loud, uncouth, unruly, and dangerous. However, even that revolutionary music genre was facing growing pains. Popular groups like the Beach Boys and the Four Seasons were being replaced by new cultural phenomena.

The American artist, Bob Dylan, made protest and political songs popular. The Grateful Dead and Jefferson Airplane were spreading the counterculture/hippy culture to teens all over the country. Black groups like the Temptations and Supremes had crossed over and were now celebrating nationwide hits. These songs had messages about politics, life, drugs, and sex. Parents often tried to prevent their kids from listening to these revolutionary anthems.

But the biggest rite of passage was from across the Atlantic. The British invasion had won the music war led by the Beatles generals: John, Paul, George, and Ringo.

These new cultural influences often bumped up against old ones.

SPANKING VS. SPOCKING

Wholesale differences between how children of the Depression were raised and the new rules for raising the postwar baby boomers were also probably responsible for the coming generation gap.

In the early twentieth century a well-adjusted adult was supposed to be a creature of habit and self-control. As a result, child rearing stressed the importance of imposing regular habits on infants. Mothers were discouraged from kissing their babies, told to ignore their crying and to break such habits as thumb sucking. Discipline was in. The nonsmiling faces of Aaron and Mary were exactly like both of my grandmothers' (ironically also named Mary) whose "smiles" struck fear in the heart of all of my cousins and myself.

Harry was a product of that ethos and of his cultural traditions. First-generation immigrants, usually working class, tended to be stricter disciplinarians. Children's emerging personalities were subordinated to families' needs with little demonstrable affection or praise. The premium was on obedience. However, as a Jewish family, the Greissmans also had middle-class aspirations like education, independence, and self-direction.

The majority of Eastern European Jewish families who came to the United States were nominally Orthodox. They were not, though, among the most learned or pious of that generation. Nevertheless, they held on to a distinctive Jewish ethos and way of life. The husband was the dominant spouse, the primary breadwinner, and the master of the house, at least in theory. Yet, quite often, the wife was forced to work or be in the family business where both husband and wife often worked together. The needs of the group, especially one's family, generally took precedence over any one of its members.

Thousands of immigrant children were removed from school to work in sweatshops or to perform other menial labor in order to guarantee their family's subsistence income.

They, as adults, were to remain as working-class folk, destined to raise their kids in the more traditional manner. As parents, they would be more likely to use the same strict, sometimes corporal, disciplinarian methods as their parents.

Paradoxically the personal achievement of boys and men was also encouraged, with the hope that the rewards would benefit the entire family. Maybe that is why the Greissman family sacrificed Harry's immediate income potential for a future based on a college education. Harry was 22 and single when he graduated college in 1937. The repercussions of the Depression and the coming war certainly robbed his immediate family of what they may have hoped for, but his future family was to benefit in more ways than just financial from this gift of higher education. How he was to raise his kids had to also have been greatly affected by his higher education.

Richard and Jamie were born in 1950 and 1953, Allan in 1961. Postwar parenting had become very different in middle-class families. Many war-weary parents, especially the college educated, were scornful of the strict child-rearing methods of their parents and grandparents. They embraced the advice of Dr. Benjamin Spock, who advocated the loss of strict disciplinary methods, rigid feeding, bathing, and sleeping schedules, and told parents to pick up their babies and enjoy them. Spock's 1946 book, *Baby and Childcare* became the parenting bible. By the time Jamie was born in 1953 it had already sold five million copies. Spock, more than any other individual of his time, reshaped the child-rearing process. Maybe that's why Jamie became a psychologist.

Spock was more concerned with children's feelings and natural urges to sleep, eat, and have their own potty time. This brought on a greater rejection of reward and punishment and less fear of spoiling. Children received more cuddling, holding, affection, and understanding. It brought on moderation in punishment, yet maintained the idea that rewards and penalties were essential for effective disciplining even after more progressive democratic conflict resolution techniques were used.[86] Middle-class and college-educated parents like Harry and Iris raised their children to value achievement, initiative, and personal responsibility.

Harry and Iris were not of the same generation. First-generation working-class immigrants who were stricter disciplinarians brought up Harry. Harry's college experiences tempered him. That her older sister also raised Iris tempered her. That combination affected the family.

Thus, Harry and Iris, like many other parents of the 1950s, emphasized Spock's methods and postwar parenting goals of conformity, gender role identity, material success, yet the oddly conflicting trait of independence. That trait would also lead to the famous generation gap to come. What would also lead to a greater generation gap was the changing view about women's roles in a family, work, and society.

Harry could, even with his tendency to be personally risk-averse, be confident in all three of his children. So, for instance, a week after Richard got his driver's permit he did not object when Iris suggested Richard drive them all to Joe and Ruth's house. Harry could have easily said no, it's too soon, but didn't. It is a great example of when he said to his children—quietly or silently—I believe in you, I trust you can do this. I did so and so at your age. So can you. Cousin Arnold (by then a lawyer) told them later that unfortunately Richard had actually driven illegally because they had gone out of the area where he could legally drive with his permit (Westchester County)—across Bronx and Queens (New York City) to get to Woodmere.

Harry the dedicated tennis player, was also a baseball fan who played it in his youth and while in the army. Richard, as most American boys of the era, grew up playing Little League baseball. Harry went to Richard's games when they didn't conflict with his tennis games. Richard recalls that Harry was ecstatic when he once hit a triple that flew well over the left fielder's head and was the farthest he had ever hit a ball.

But, Harry could also flash his temper to protect his son. Richard often was the leadoff batter. The coach of one team, whose son was the pitcher, wanted to intimidate Richard's team by hitting the first batter with a pitch. It was very obvious to everyone that the "wild" pitch that hit Richard in the jaw was deliberately thrown at the batter. Harry was furious. He went with Richard's coach and protested to the umpire. Remember that parents are supposed to stay in the stands and let the coaches deal with the umpires and protest of that nature. Did Harry's father ever come watch Harry play anything, let alone fight for him? I sincerely doubt it. This was Harry being the more modern dad.

WHEN I'M 64

The times, indeed, were "a changin'" for Harry as well as the world. By the late 1960s he was climbing toward his professional peak. Two decades later, he would be retired.

David Ogilvy states that anyone who wants to rise to the top in advertising must be ambitious.

A person can get by just being the go between men, but in order to gain power, you have to have more aspirations.[87]

Harry was not the ambitious type. As someone whose formative years took place during the Depression, he was more concerned with stability and security rather than ambition that might require switching or losing jobs. He always had a job that paid decently, but never was he a top paid guy. He was safe. His family was secure. That was what mattered.

The 1960s looked like a very good decade for Harry. In 1964 he attended a "Voyage to India" reception featuring a designer fashion show of Indian-inspired creations in honor of B. K. Nehru, wife of the Indian ambassador to the Unites States hosted by *McCall's* Magazine. In 1968, Lew Zale, the executive vice president of the Zale Corporation, thanked Harry for notifying him of the CLIO award won at the American and Radio Television Festival. The CLIOs are awards given for innovation and creative excellence in advertising. It was named after the Greek goddess Clio, the mythological muse known as "the proclaimer, glorifier and celebrator of history, great deeds and accomplishments."[88]

These 1968 photos taken by a Japanese associate show Harry with a Japanese executive and an award the looks suspiciously like a CLIO. That same year Harry hosted another Japanese executive and his kimono-dressed wife at his home. It looked like things were going very well for Harry.

By March 1970, he had become director of creative services for Vick International and was a member of the executive board of the annual Advertising Club of NY ANDY Awards Competition that had been founded in 1964.

Later that year, as reported by *Advertising Age*, he was promoted to director of marketing services and according to the magazine, Iris Greissman wasn't happy that Harry "missed her birthday [July 30] for the fifth consecutive year—and three of those were due to his attendance at the Chicago event." The Advertising Age Creative Workshop.

It had taken him twenty some odd years to get to this point. Another "unspoken" reason a man with Harry's talents did not rise through the ranks faster or higher was anti-Semitism.

In non-Jewish-owned firms, like Vick International, Jews were relegated to "creative positions" during the 1950s and early 1960s and not allowed into management ranks for years. Even *Mad Men* showed this. Harry's nephew Arnie strongly believes that this is the main reason Harry didn't move up faster.

Here, he looked quite comfortable in this undated Mad Man *photo.*

In 1975, Richardson-Vicks moved from the Chanin building, a roughly fifty-minute commute by train, to a brand new facility built on a densely wooded site in Wilton, Connecticut, a drive of approximately the same length.

The problem with this move, besides changing a routine Harry had been used to for approximately twenty-five years, was that to everyone's worry, Harry now had to drive a car to work.

Harry and Iris finally needed a second car. They had purchased cars for their two oldest children, Richard and Jamie. People's cars often symbolize their personalities. Richard had a used safe and conservative Volvo station wagon, and Jamie a fast and hot Buick V-8 Skylark. What did Iris buy for Harry? An AMC Hornet nicknamed the "Green Hornet." It was short, stocky, and cheap, in case he wrecked it.

I married Jamie late in 1974 and in 1976 was laid off, along with 15,000 other NYC teachers. Harry offered me a temporary job editing old Vicks TV commercials into historical archive reels. Those were the only times I visited his workplace. I wasn't there for more than it took to complete the task, yet from time to time I was able to share lunch with him at the cafeteria. We would politely chat about work and politics, but he was still a private person. I always found it hard to talk to him.

As a teacher and lover of history, I tried over the years to get him to talk about his World War II experiences, or to use his writing talents to tell his story. It was no use. He didn't even tell me about the documents he had in his possession. We found those by accident as we cleaned up what he left behind. It became my duty to tell his story.

Nine years after the company moved, Harry moved closer to work, to Yorktown Heights and we bought the house at 10 Kenneth. Originally, their plan was to sell it and move nearer to work when Harry's company moved. However, Allan was just about to start high school, so Harry sacrificed. Despite him being a horrible driver, he commuted each day to the office.

At that point in time he did not look like a man still enjoying his job. Perhaps it was the driving. Perhaps it was being one of the oldest on staff. Perhaps it was a feeling that he was not as essential as he once was. Sixty plus year old ad men, unless a partner or top executive, were usually eased out of work and prepared for the exit door.

Finally, after "14,080 days around the world," Harry bid farewell to his career.

By his side? His partner in life at that point for thirty-five years, Iris.

PAYING IT FORWARD

At this point in time, he and Iris, who still worked, wanted to spend more time wintering in Florida. Yet it seemed that Harry was searching for more ways to keep busy and go back to his creative days. He had always done freelance work for his buddies Danny Abraham who owned Slimfast, and Walter Zachen, who owned Standard Lumber in Elizabeth, New Jersey. Upon retirement, he wanted to do additional freelance creative work for his friends. His work led to some quid pro quo. When Jamie and I wanted to build a new deck at 10 Kenneth, I rented a very large teamster-sized truck and picked up the discounted lumber at Walter's place in Elizabeth, New Jersey. Good thing my dad drove an eighteen-wheel big rig. Maybe it was in the blood.

According to Allan, although Weight Watchers had a lock on the dieting market, Slimfast was hot on its tail. For a while it was a popular product. Harry did some freelance advertising for them and may have invested a small amount in the company as well. Danny was actually a former student of Harry's at Baruch College who was so impressed he asked Harry to do some work for him. They became lifelong friends. Harry and Iris took a dream trip to Israel because of Danny's "connections" there.

He also did product development and advertising for a neighbor (Ben Amato) who was a principal oboist in the Metropolitan Opera orchestra. Ben invented a machine that could carve the double reed used by oboists to the user's specification. Harry came up with the name *Perfect-a-Reed* and did the promotional advertising for Ben's invention. For a few years, on weekends (after tennis) Harry, Iris, and Allan even sold madras shirts from India at the Yonkers Raceway Flea Market that they got from a son of Harry and Iris's friends, the Matthews. They never sold too many, although I bought a couple. They were actually fashionable at the time. Maybe.

Harry was also a born teacher. Throughout much of his career, until his company moved to Connecticut, he taught advertising and marketing at Baruch College and Fordham University's School of Business where he was known as a very dynamic, prolific, energetic, tough, and creative instructor. Perhaps the experience of teaching artillery methods during the war inspired him. I always thought he would be a great teacher of writing.

The students loved him, but he was tough grading them. He rarely gave As, but he certainly got Danny Abraham's attention.

Richard remembers observing,

> *The class was all older students, working professionals who were going back to do graduate work. Probably the most remarkable thing about the class I remember was inventiveness. His assignments were always so clever. One in particular that struck me that was really fun. My dad introduced the assignment by saying: "Imagine you had to do a promotional campaign for a fountain pen that took in water but wrote in ink." The other thing was how flamboyant he was in the classroom.*
>
> *He was a pretty reserved guy, not particularly flashy, and yet there were two notable exceptions: how he behaved with strangers—he always seemed to encourage conversation with strangers at the tennis court or flirt with waitresses in restaurants. He would make a comment about how pretty she was or how she fixed her hair—very playful. In the classroom, he had this kind of Walter Middy personality. He was sparkling, impish, very dramatic and theatrical. Part of teaching advertising and promotion was being promotional. He was comfortable in the classroom, role modeling how to be promotional. It was about him—he was the center of attention. In the classroom, he was a little narcissistic and certainly did not share the spotlight. His students really enjoyed him, so I don't think it was not just for my benefit. There was a rapport with his students already and it didn't seem to be just about entertaining me. I loved watching him teach. He was very good at it. It certainly nurtured in me an interest in teaching.*

Why was he so outgoing with strangers? Where was that guy at home? Why, there, did he retreat within himself? Which was the act and which was the real Harry? How much of who Harry had become was formed in the events of his childhood in Brooklyn, being a teenager and college student during the Depression, and a wounded veteran of World War II?

In January 1968 Baruch thanked Harry for twenty years of teaching in their evening division where, "many hundreds of students have gained from you both knowledge and inspiration." Additionally, the certificate said, "By your collective efforts, you have helped to enrich the New York Community."

When Richard and Jamie were in junior high school, the Ardsley School District had just opened its youth center and announced a contest to name the center. Harry was sitting with them and he suddenly said, "What about 'Five Hive'?" (the district was School District #5) and exclaimed that the youth center is like a hive with all its activities. "His eyes sparkled with excitement." Jamie submitted the name and it won. Although we don't know if she asked him to create the slogan for her, she certainly took the credit.

That isn't all Harry did. Although not a great "community" guy, he was part of the local Temple Beth Abraham community. That was probably more Iris's doing as she became the temple administrator there. Allan thinks Harry rode in on Iris's coat tails. In addition to being a member of the congregation, he used his talents to work on their calendar journal and worked for B'nai B'rith. Even before that, he was selected to be president of the Saw Mill River Lodge of B'nai B'rith.

Although no longer a formally practicing Orthodox Jew, this was one way Harry gave back. When Beth Abraham's rabbi would take vacation in the summer, Harry was one of the men who stood in as rabbi. He would read from the Torah and lead the prayers. Leading the service probably brought him back to a childhood memory of going to synagogue. Richard distinctly remembers how his brothers referred to him by his Hebrew name, "Herschel," not Harry. He loved being called that—and it was always said with a tone of warmth by both Sol and Lou.

These activities, in 20-20 hindsight, allowed him to show off his abilities that at home weren't part of the day-to-day realities of Iris's household.

Jamie remembers that

> *Harry was raised orthodox and the connection to temple was important to him. Being next to him at services was always punctuated by his very poor singing of the "Sh'ma." At one point, the lyric is supposed to be pronounced "u sh'ma, u sh'ma." But each time that line would come up, he would turn to us and even more loudly sing, "you Schmo, you Schmo." [Schmo is a Yiddish/English slang term for an uninteresting man, or in some circles, a schmuck.] Even now, I always laugh or tear up when I hear that hymn.*

Harry just had a knack of getting involved with perfect strangers resulting in quid pro quos. He would start conversations with strangers and the next thing you knew he was doing something for them. One example was at the local radio station, WFAS. He met Jon Yatts, a radio announcer there, and ended up writing ad copy for them. In return, Yatts set up a high school internship for Richard.

One interesting story of Harry helping a perfect stranger comes from Paul Feiner, the Greenburgh town supervisor. Greenburgh is the largest town in Westchester County, New York. However, it is a rather odd place. It has no post office of its own. In fact, it has seven zip codes. It is composed of unincorporated areas that include the hamlet of Hartsdale (with a post office and includes 10 Kenneth's zip code) and Edgemont (which is only a school district). Within its boundaries are the villages of Ardsley, Dobbs Ferry, Elmsford, Hastings-on-Hudson, Irvington, and Tarrytown.

To either clarify or further confuse anyone, 10 Kenneth Road had a Hartsdale zip code, was in the Ardsley school district, and was provided police, fire, sanitation, road, park, and recreation services by Greenburgh. Got that? I came to call it "Arsdaleburgh." Anyway, back to Paul Feiner, in his own words.

> *I remember meeting Harry Greissman sometime around 1983. I was running for election as County Legislator and was knocking on doors [his included]. I recall the conversations I had back then. I was running for election against Tom Abinanti, a*

Greenburgh Town Board member. I was the outsider, was perceived to have little or no chance of winning. Although I was active in community activities for a number of years before running for Legislator, I was considered by most people to be a gadfly, not taken seriously by the political establishment.

Harry was one of the few initial supporters who encouraged me. I remember most of my initial supporters—because there were so few of them. And remember having many conversations with him during the course of my campaign—and also remember his volunteer efforts on my behalf which helped me win my office.

I remember Harry telling me to be myself. He and others helped me come up with winning initial strategies. One of my first slogans was: "Choose Paul Feiner or Get a Politician."

As in today's world, people did not trust politicians. Many promises made by political candidates were broken. I received lots of attention with a concept that we talked about: a money back guarantee. I also posted my home phone number on literature and encouraged people to call me till midnight. If I made a promise and broke it, the campaign contributors would get their money back. This promise received national attention—even though most politicians hated the concept. Harry helped me come up with these concepts, [and helped me] highlight those issues that I had worked on before running for office that meant something to the voters:

- *My successful efforts getting a bus service started from Westchester to NYC.*
- *Getting women admitted as members of the Scarsdale Town Club—a club that selected the mayor.*
- *The county closing the Bronx River Parkway for cyclists and the county appropriating funds for bikeways.*

Most of all, I remember that Harry was a terrific person. Easy to talk to. Very accessible. He made me feel important (even if I wasn't) and was always constructive. I don't think I would be where I am today without his help.

—Paul Feiner, Greenburgh Town Supervisor

Everyman and The Generation Gap

Richard, Jamie, and even Allan, as baby boomers were becoming part of a new generation, more and more split from Harry's. When Richard and Jamie were both in high school, Harry was 50 plus. There had always been growing pains for teens, but in the 1960s this pain became a calling. Sixties teens weren't supposed to "trust anyone over 30." Like many 1960s families with teens becoming adults during this time, this generation gap became more pronounced.

It seems Harry was, in many ways, the "everydad" of his generation. Work consumed his existence. As a parent he was more hands-off than hands-on. He was a good man, who worked hard, did everything he could to provide for his family, and always was proud of their achievements. That being said, it may not be so strange that Jamie doesn't have many memories of him, other than him being home, smoking his pipe or cigar, or sneaking an occasional cigarette, reading the paper, watching some TV, and going off to play tennis.

Following the typical family mold of two parents and two, then three, kids, Iris was the queen bee of the household. Iris loved to shop, and money was always an issue between her and miserly Harry. She loved to buy things for the house, which would displease Harry to no end. In addition to working, she usually took care of the house (other than a cleaning woman once a week who may have been certifiably crazy, and "balabustaring" Jamie), bought the food, prepared the meals, took the kids places, paid the bills, and actively asserted her opinions in everyone's lives. She shared some information about the kids with Harry, but he didn't get involved in much of their daily lives, unless she was really angry with them and wanted him to play "bad cop" pop. This was her world. Harry knew it and stayed outside of it unless called on.

How much of this dynamic was due to the environments in which Harry and Iris grew up, and how much of it was due to their individual personalities? Whatever the causes,

Harry was more detached. It was probably a generational thing, but Iris's power and individual strength had a great deal to do with that detachment as well.

My mom was the boss of the family, the disciplinarian; she ran the household, paid the bills, organized much of our life. My dad worked real hard, loved to come home and read and play tennis. One of the great loves they shared was card playing, in particular bridge. They weren't particularly physical with each other—they would kiss, but he was very reserved and quiet typically. Iris would be busy in the kitchen or cleaning. Her biggest hobby was listening to music while she was busy with household stuff. She was the parent who made sure the family saw relatives, made plans for outings like going to the movies or plays or concerts as a family. Iris would take Harry and the kids to the movies. Harry was more like one of the kids. He loved to laugh a rich and warm laugh in the theatre.

—Richard

As a young adult coming back from the war, Harry had made a series of fateful decisions similar to many men of his Greatest Generation. Forty years later was he, like so many others, looking back and thinking what if?

He chose to be a jewelry store manager and not a cub reporter for a newspaper. He chose to stay with the same company for 39 years rather than seek other opportunities even though he was an enormously talented individual. He rarely read fiction as an adult even though he was such a student of literature growing up. He never wrote that novel. Why? Had his Depression upbringing shaped him? Had the war changed him? Had his need for security and safety for his new family guided him?

Like many other suburban men his age, he had also become very comfortable in a life that had very powerful routines. Weekdays he woke up, went to work, returned home, ate dinner, read, and watched some TV. On the weekends he played as much tennis as he could and maintained the lawn and flowers. He weeded. He watered. He planted "packasandra" and fussed over it regularly. He enjoyed being outside, secretively smoking there.

Harry became the "everyman" suburban commuter. His daily train schedule, his one or two nights per week teaching, and his tennis routinized his life. He didn't help clean up after dinner, never cooked, never did laundry (except for the tennis clothes or jock he urgently needed), and was generally removed from what was going on in the household. He was loving, but not emotional. He would hug and kiss the kids, but rarely say, "I love you."

He was patient at times, but could be extremely intolerant and inpatient, depending on his mood and what they were doing. He hated when the kids would argue, or fight, and would raise his voice in exasperation. He never cursed (other than the famous Broccoli joke— which made it all the more funny—until it was overdone!). He would just say "Damn it" when really mad. But did he want more? Was he happy or was he disappointed in himself? How typical was he of the men of his times?

As in many other families, Harry's weekend sport led to some strains. He did try to get the kids and Iris to share his passion for tennis, but perhaps too hard. Jamie recalls his being very hard on her while giving her lessons. While a great teacher of strangers, he was not very patient with family members. He would wince, raise his voice, and seem quite irritated when Jamie or Richard made errors. They soon learned to hate tennis. Richard shares this story.

> *My father and I played tennis tournaments together at Ardsley Country Club. They were particularly problematic in my senior year in high school when I was playing my best tennis, but the tournaments were often on the weekend and so were after Friday nights when I would go out to a local tavern with my friends. The drinking age was 18 then. Because I was a social drinker and most often a designated driver, on one particular Friday night my friends schemed to get me really drunk—and succeeded. I woke up the next morning really hung over, with my belly sloshing with beer. It was all my dad could do to keep his temper because we had a big tournament to play.*
>
> *I knew it was going to be a long match when with every step my head pounded and my reflexes so badly compromised. I can remember taking the first serve and thinking as the ball came at me that even if I was not hung over I couldn't get it in time. I remember just reaching out to catch the ball and saying, "Nice serve." My dad was not happy. He told me he was not happy by the look he gave me and he snarled something. Later in the game when I was in the backcourt, and my opponent hit a particularly wide shot, I went for it and hit a rather good shot ... into my dad's back while he was at the net. We didn't talk on the way home. He wasn't angry that I played badly. He got angry that I got drunk and compromised my ability to hold up the doubles team. He was a very competitive tennis player.*
>
> *Against that background, I have many more fond memories of how proud my dad was of my tennis as my game matured. It's fair to say that it was the thing he enjoyed most doing with me and we had a lot of fun. How can I tell what it was like being there? While he was not an effusive fellow, I could tell how he swelled when we played together. It was his way of bonding—of doing a father/son thing. Not much in the way of words exchanged, but a fraternity nevertheless.*

As a result of Harry's intensity Jamie didn't really want to play. Ironically, Jamie introduced the game to me. It has become our family game. She plays tennis several times a week if possible. She has become passionate, plays hard, and competitively. In fact, one reason we chose our new condominium, a scant three miles from 10 Kenneth, was the tennis court in our backyard. Of course we joke that it is our property, but it is actually part of the community where we now live. Harry would have undoubtedly approved. She feels Harry on the court with her and knows he would be proud.

On the other hand, Jamie would turn to Harry for occasional help with homework, particularly English assignments. He had an incredible amount of knowledge about classics, poetry, and authors. He was a walking literary encyclopedia. When he was asked to help with writing, he was a virtual thesaurus, yet he, too impatient to help with rewrites, tended to just rewrite. Now, Jamie admits submitting his work because, "It was just so much better." He did not usually initiate conversation, or ask her about her life, friends, boyfriends, and interests, but she knew that if she told him something, he usually listened, might ask some questions, and might even give an opinion. She recalls another Harry tactic,

> *My father, in his subtle manner, made it clear that complaining about school or teachers or a variety of things that seem unfair to many kids, was not something he took lightly. I remember that if I ever had a complaint about anything to do with school, (or even anything not school related!) he had a stock response. He would listen, would say something like, "Oh that's too bad," and then proceed with his wry statement of "I'll write a letter to Dr. Johnson."*
>
> *Now, Dr. Johnson was the Superintendent of Schools, and was in that position for many years. He was an older Southern gentleman, who was "old school." The thought that my father would write a letter, and that I might be called in to the Superintendent's office to discuss my beef, shut me up quickly.*
>
> *In fact, the letter to Dr. Johnson was about as overdone as the Broccoli joke. My brothers and I knew that as soon as dad went to that tactic, we rescinded any complaint. Pretty smart parenting style—pretend to be supportive in a way that made us reconsider our position!*

Richard took French in high school and was given an assignment to read a book of poems by Charles Baudelaire. Harry looked at the book, looked at the poem Richard was reading and sighed, "Oh if only if you could hear this in French." He didn't offer to read it in French, but Richard was so impressed and proud that his dad was fluent enough in a language to be able to read it in the original.

As many from his generation, Harry had a thing about spending money, and seemed clueless about the cost of household items. He had a real Depression mentality about spending and would wince if he knew how much something cost. He was thrifty, to say the least, and never passed up taking something that was free, or available. He had come out of a childhood that was economically precarious; his family was desperately poor. For him and his generation, security was so important.

Richard recalls:

> *I remember one particular time when after a year of living at home—before graduate school—I used some of my savings to buy my first SLR camera and two lenses. I chose not to get kit lenses though they would be less expensive because I wanted good lenses to go with my first real camera. I asked my Uncle Sol for advice and he agreed, notably saying I should stay away from zoom lenses that were what you typically got with the kit.*
>
> *Foolishly, that evening, I left my camera box and lenses on the kitchen table along with the receipt. My dad saw the amount I spent on the camera and was furious at me. As he does when he yelled, he got very red faced and demanded to know why I spent so much money. Even though he knew it was my money, it was to his mind inexcusable spending.*

But it's the way he always reacted when any family member spent a lot of money on something they loved and could defend. But his reaction was from a much deeper well. It was a reaction of someone in particular a man of his generation who on the one hand through hard work and talent and a healthy dollop of good luck had been successful but was still haunted by the insecurities of childhood and the fear that all they had accumulated might somehow be lost.

The 1960s counter revolution, the feminist movement, and its music also brought about a revolution in fashion. Blue jeans replaced dress pants or chinos. Facial hair grew. Then again so did the length of men's hair. Women became freer in expressing their sexuality. They even went braless. Harry looked askew at how Richard and Jamie were being transformed by the new era. He hated rock and roll, but other than asking them to lower the volume, never made a fuss … usually.

Harry hated much of the music Richard listened to, "I remember we watched *Ed Sullivan* together—the Doors came on to perform their song 'Touch Me,' and when I asked him what he thought, he said that at least there was 'some music' in the segment (the interlude with strings). He hated the Doors and those 'damn' Beatles!!"

"That confounded music" and "hideous and revealing" clothing became areas of contention between generations as the new generation strove for more independence. Dress and skirt hems grew higher and higher to the point of many a dad saying, "You will not leave my house dressed like that."

http://oliviamarie06.tripod.com/sixtyclothes.htm

Jamie was allowed to wear short mini dresses. She doesn't remember Harry commenting on her clothing as a teenager. He never seemed to mind, but as she said, "I do think he noticed." He left it to Iris to decide what was okay and to set limits on Jamie's clothing, makeup, or activities. Richard was not an issue. He never wore skirts.

Richard and Jamie were approaching college and adulthood. Richard graduated from high school in 1969, Jamie in 1971. Although heavily influenced by growing up in the 1960s, they were not counterculture kids. They were generally straight and successful in school. Richard was elected to his school's Student Council.

Mischievous Jamie, who finally developed good impulse control, was a school "leader" working with administrators, not protesting against them. One of her big adventures was to try smoking cigarettes with her friend Donna by sticking their heads out the bathroom window as to not leave the telltale smell indoors. Yeah, that worked.

Richard looked and acted as the proverbial middle of the road, middle-class, successful high school student. Neither seemed that interested or involved in the politics of the time, outside of high school. They were admitted to Colgate and Skidmore Colleges.

NEW STUDENT COUNCIL OFFICERS STATE PLANS FOR NEXT YEAR

STUDENT COUNCIL Officers for next year Rich Greissman, Janet Burgess, Fred Kaplan

That's Richard on the left.

When Richard came home or when he took a year off after graduating from Colgate with his bachelor's degree, he and Harry would watch *Kung-Fu* on TV and black-and-white silent films (Buster Keaton, Charlie Chaplin). "Dad would laugh so hard that Mom would stop her work in the kitchen to come to the head of the stairs and watch the two of us together." That Harry shared something from his era with Richard was one of Richard's fondest memories.

Richard and Harry would watch Shakespearian productions on TV and enjoy them together. They shared a love of Alfred Hitchcock. They both enjoyed *Amos 'n' Andy* on TV, odd, given Richard's hatred of racism. Harry would tell Richard how important radio was for him growing up. Laurel and Hardy was a favorite, but Richard enjoyed the Three Stooges more. Harry loved Westerns. They were a mainstay of 1950s and early 1960s movie making. They talked about how much they enjoyed *The Magnificent Seven*—the theme of courage, of righting a wrong, standing up to bullies—but also that it was a mixture of toughness and tenderness. That 1960 movie adapted from an earlier Japanese film about seven samurais is a great metaphor for America's role in the Cold War, coming to the aid of "innocent" foreigners controlled by an evil dictatorship.

During Richard's first year at Colgate, he had a full year requirement of taking two courses involving philosophy, religion, and drama. The first semester was thematically organized around the Old Testament and the second semester around the New Testament. Richard steeped himself not only in the five books of Moses, but also in some of the great philosophers of Jewish thought, including Maimonides and Martin Buber.

Harry was thrilled when at Thanksgiving and at December holidays Richard shared his studies in Jewish thought and the somewhat playful paper he wrote about Job whom he characterized as a reluctant existentialist. Harry would listen, and didn't so much advance the conversation as he signaled how proud he was of Richard's intellectual work. Maybe as a reward, Harry introduced Richard to one of his favorite pastimes—a tumbler of Johnny Walker Red after dinner. Richard admits he even dabbled with pipe smoking as more homage to his dad.

In thinking back on Harry's love of literature, particularly poetry, and how it influenced his own intellectual development, Richard remembers the time that Harry and he had a particularly ugly fight about the truthfulness of some claim. They disagreed, argued, even yelled vehemently. It was a sign of a new time. As was Harry's habit in times like this, he stormed off to sulk. Richard felt really badly and struggled to think of a way to make things right. He grabbed a notecard and wrote the words "Beauty is truth, truth beauty. That is all ye need to know on earth. That is all ye need to know," the last few lines of Keats's poem on seeing the Elgin Marble. Harry understood the purpose of the card and they hugged.

EVE OF DESTRUCTION

"Eve of Destruction"
A song by Barry McGuire
The eastern world it is exploding
Violence flarin', bullets loadin'
You're old enough to kill but not for votin'
You don't believe in war but what's that gun you're totin'?
And even the Jordan River has bodies floatin'

But you tell me
Over and over and over again my friend
Ah, you don't believe
We're on the eve of destruction

Don't you understand what I'm tryin' to say
Can't you feel the fears I'm feelin' today?
If the button is pushed, there's no runnin' away
There'll be no one to save with the world in a grave
Take a look around you boy, it's bound to scare you boy

And you tell me
Over and over and over again my friend
Ah, you don't believe
We're on the eve of destruction

Yeah my blood's so mad feels like coagulating
I'm sitting here just contemplatin'

153

I can't twist the truth it knows no regulation
Handful of senators don't pass legislation
And marches alone can't bring integration
When human respect is disintegratin'
This whole crazy world is just too frustratin'

And you tell me
Over and over and over again my friend
Ah, you don't believe
We're on the eve of destruction

Think of all the hate there is in Red China
Then take a look around to Selma, Alabama
You may leave here for four days in space
But when you return it's the same old place
The pounding of the drums, the pride and disgrace
You can bury your dead but don't leave a trace
Hate your next-door neighbor but don't forget to say grace

And tell me
Over and over and over and over again my friend
You don't believe
We're on the eve of destruction
Mmm, no, no, you don't believe
We're on the eve of destruction

Written by P. F. Sloan, Steve Barri. Copyright © Universal Music Publishing Group.

That song startled everyone, old and young alike. It spoke of the fear and anxieties during that period. It should probably be re-released now in 2017.

There were so many serious things for parents to worry about. The Civil Rights Movement had turned more violent. Television exposed more of the horrors of segregation, anti-Black violence, and bigotry in the south. Even though there had been progress made, such as President Johnson's historic War on Poverty and the Voting Rights Act of 1965, the lack of economic progress and de facto segregation led to mid-1960s riots in cities all across the nation. Martin Luther King's dreams were not being realized quickly enough.

Black nationalist groups such as the Black Muslims and the Black Panthers stressed, in the words of Malcolm X, actions "by any means necessary" and less dependency on the White approach. Racial discrimination and repression remained a significant factor in American life. Even after Dr. King initiated a Poor People's Campaign in 1968, the distribution of the nation's wealth and income moved toward greater inequality. May saw his assassination.

The Vietnam War exploded with over one million American soldiers involved. It became the most divisive issue during the era, even among family members. World War II and Korean War Veterans often could not understand why their sons were rebellious "antipatriotic" traitors by not supporting the war and in some cases avoiding the draft. Why was this war so different? Harry had a son of age for the draft. He was a father first. He never wanted his son to go through what he had gone through twenty-five years earlier.

Why were we involved in the affairs of a little Southeast Asian nation so far away?

Southeast Asia had been a French colony. The French were defeated in 1954 by Ho Chi Minh and his communist Viet Minh party. Following the removal of the French, Vietnam was divided into the Communist North led by Ho and the "democratic" South, with the United States as its defender. This was the Cold War, with the North as a Soviet and Chinese surrogate. The war began when each side wanted to reunite the country as either a Communist or Democratic republic. Within South Vietnam the Viet Cong, northern supported opponents, grew in numbers.

In 1961, working under the Cold War's "domino theory," which held that if one Communist country fell to communism, many would follow, Kennedy increased US aid. By 1962, the US military presence in South Vietnam had reached some 9,000 "advisor" troops, compared with fewer than 800 during the 1950s. By 1969, at the peak of US involvement in the war, more than 500,000 US military personnel were involved in the Vietnam conflict. By the time the United States withdrew from the war, in 1973, more than 3 million people were killed in the Vietnam War.

"One out of every 10 Americans who served in Vietnam was a casualty. Over 58,000 were killed and 304,000 wounded out of 2.7 million who served. Although the percent that died is similar to other wars, amputations or crippling wounds were 300 percent higher than in World War II. 75,000 Vietnam veterans are severely disabled."[89]

People across the nation at first thought it our duty to support the effort as part of the Cold War. However, as more and more US troops were drafted and sent overseas, overwhelming support, especially by young people, turned into everything from disap-

http://blogs.mprnews.org/newscut/2014/10/
on-50th-anniversary-a-sanitized-vietnam-war/

http://www.cnn.com/2013/07/01/world/vietnam-war-fast-facts/

pointment in the policies to violent protest. Arguments against it ranged from whether or not it was our role to intervene in another nation's internal struggle to whether or not we should police the world to why we were killing innocent Vietnamese.

Television, as it had about racism in the Southern United States now televised the war's mayhem and destruction, leading many more to ask why. Even worse, we were killing our boys (average age 19) in a war we shouldn't be involved in at all.

http://www.nbcnews.com/news/other/vietnam-war-photos-still-powerful-nearly-50-years-later-f8C11404994

The war also had civil rights implications. A far greater percentage of minorities fought and died in Vietnam than their percentage of the US population. Martin Luther King protested it. Heavyweight Champion Mohammed Ali lost his boxing license because he refused to serve, as a conscientious objector. This finally led to a change in the draft laws, eliminating the deferments mostly used by young white males, and replacing it with a draft lottery based on birthdays. That had a huge impact on American families. Even more turned against the war as more white sons, brothers, and husbands were now in greater danger.

The elimination of Richard's college deferment that made him 100 percent eligible for the draft shook Harry. Luckily neither Richard nor I were drafted. We all watched the drawings of the lottery numbers on TV on December 1, 1969. It was the strangest Bingo game I ever played. On that night the first of 366 blue plastic capsules with birthday days on litmus paper were picked out of a topless birdcage by an obscure Republican Congressman from New York, Alexander R. Pirnie. One. By. One. We waited until ours turned up. The first birthdate drawn that night, assigned the lowest number, "001," was September 14. This went on for seven years.

My lottery number was 348 out of 366. Richard's was 150. Harry remembered war so much he forgot it all.

To say the least, the 1960s were problematic to families trying to raise children and keep them safe. Protests, both peaceful and not, sprung up across the nation. Lyndon Johnson walked away from the presidency as a result of the war. Robert F. Kennedy, a leading contender to be the Democratic Party's candidate for president was also assassinated a month after the assassination of Dr. King. Political turmoil raged at the 1968 Democratic National Convention in Chicago. Hundreds of thousands protested the war in Washington.

http://www.vietnow.com/draft-lottery/

http://www.lib.berkeley.edu/MRC/pacificaviet.html. http://www.cnn.
com/2014/05/02/us/gallery/kent-state-shooting/

At Ohio's Kent State University, National Guardsmen shot and killed four students in 1970.

Where did Harry stand on these issues? Free speech was a big issue. The rights to dissent and present more controversial materials in schools became part of the era. When Richard was a junior in high school there was such a free speech controversy. An English teacher was in trouble because he allowed students to do something "controversial" in the school's yearbook. There was a meeting of parents in the high school auditorium. Harry got up and gave a speech in support of the teacher and the notion of free speech. I am both impressed and surprised.

Harry was a conservative Democrat, who struggled with the social issues of the day. Although he had spoken up for free speech at that parents' meeting, he was equally upset that Richard was reading Eldridge Cleaver's *Soul on Ice*. Richard sympathized with Cleaver's arguments about institutional racism, oppression, and racial separation so he and Harry argued about it.

Harry, like many of his generation, was an assimilationist—the ideas came from very personal experience with anti-Semitism throughout his life. He and his brother Sol almost changed their last name so it wasn't so obviously Jewish. Although he sympathized with the outsider status blacks had in this country, he didn't think they should be defiant. He felt that they should accept their station in life and adjust as Jews had. He put class over race as a criterion for judging people. One of the first black families to move into their Hartsdale neighborhood was acceptable because they were a very well-to-do family.

Harry was also an ardent conservative Jew when it came to issues involving Israel. He was a Zionist. He sold Israeli bonds—and he headed up any number of campaigns at temple that had to do with supporting Israel. When Richard was a junior in high school, taking US history and learning about anticommunism efforts, Harry was very comfortable with that. They did argue about McGovern, the Vietnam War and Richard's sympathies for the students at Kent State.

Does Father Still Know Best?

But Allan, dear Allan, was still a child. Ten years younger than Richard, and eight years younger than Jamie, he became "an only child" for much of the years when Richard went to Colgate in 1969 and Jamie to Skidmore in 1971 (then transferred to Penn).

Harry apparently spent some time with a very young Allan. But as Allan grew older, as did Harry, there was more and more separation, even though Allan was the only child at home for eight more years.

As he grew older, Allan became frustrated and hurt by Harry's long days and sometimes nights at work teaching. He was disappointed in not having enough time because of Harry's need for tennis. Allan was a very good athlete who played Little League baseball, local youth basketball, and even high school football, but Harry didn't have a lot of time to watch or participate. For Harry it was "tennis, tennis, tennis," although he did constantly ask Allan, as he previously asked Richard, if he was "wearing a jock strap" when he played.

Obviously, there were sibling interactions in his early childhood, but as close as Allan got to Richard, he never really got to know Jamie until he lived with her and me for a year after he graduated college.

Through the years, Harry and Allan developed a mutual love for spectator sports. They became Mets, Jets, and Knicks fans together. They went to a few Mets games and Harry even managed to take Allan to game three of the 1969 World Series.

Allan was shaped in a large part by Harry's version of fatherhood with him. Except for work, Harry didn't take him to the same places he took Richard in New York City. Instead he remembers family trips to Las Vegas or Miami to see his very successful Uncle Ash.

I bet these are worth something now.

Allan recalls that he never had a

close relationship like I had with Richard, David (me), or my son Jordan. I don't remember telling Dad "I love you" or kissing him as a teenager or young adult. I adored him as a kid but never had an emotional relationship as a teen. I think that's why I tried (try) so hard with Jordan to be there as a Dad and friend. I want him to always know I love him.

Although many years apart from when he took Richard and Jamie, Harry did take Allan to work. To Impressionable Allan, this was "an absolute delight." By this time, Harry's job had changed. He was now director of marketing services for Latin America and the Far East. Allan knew Harry traveled to these places, but the biggest treat was, as it was for Richard and Jamie, going to that Chanin building.

There, across the street from the magnificent Grand Central Station, Allan would look out the window from up high and marvel at the New York skyline and the people far below. He would also marvel at that same old Horn & Hardart. Allan would put the nickels in the slots to pay for the food from the little glass doors. Like all the other kids, with a small handful of change they could get anything they wanted. Together, Harry and he would sit anywhere, "maybe next to a pauper, a rich banker, or famous journalist." In the 1970s these magnificent but dying restaurants were slowly replaced by … wait for it … Burger Kings. Many lamented what the chain had stood for: beauty, quality, service, and cleanliness.

At Harry's work, Allan would meet people from all over the world. Amazingly, Harry would fluently respond in their many languages. Allan was never really sure exactly what Harry did, but his clients always left happy and satisfied. For Allan, Harry "had a great office with a great view, and everyone came to talk to him."

Harry did try to mentor Allan, but it seemed to be more about school. Harry wasn't great at math or science, but he was great at history, English, and Spanish. He would quiz Allan, but frustrated him and made him so tense he "could not spell the word 'the.'" He didn't mentor Allan about life, girls, business, or his future career, "but he taught me about being a good person and a hard worker." In fact,

Richard was my second father just as much as an older brother. Dad didn't teach me to shave, drive a car, the "Birds and the Bees." He didn't get me my first beer; play blackjack with me in Atlantic City when I turned 18. Those were Richard's and Mom's tasks. But in the end, I kind of figured it out. Dad taught me morals and how to treat and respect others.

Whether via direct conversation or through osmosis, Allan learned what Harry taught him well. Allan knew Harry was frugal to a fault because of growing up in the Depression. He knew both Harry and Iris worked hard for their money and to pay for things most kids took for granted. He knew Harry realized that he had three kids and a mortgage. He knew

Harry was not a gambler, nor a risk taker, that he was not the kind to take a chance and try a new job, and that he enjoyed his career and was well liked, but his sense of responsibility made him work at night. I think it was more. I think Harry wanted to teach and at doing so at night was the only way.

Allan goes on.

> *We even sold clothes made by a neighbor, Harlan Mathews, at the flea markets on Sundays. I know, for example, that my mother sold her engagement ring to help pay for my Bar Mitzvah.*

Harry in one of those shirts.

From all this Allan learned a sense of entrepreneurism.

> *I worked hard as a kid. I didn't want to live "impoverished" to use a word. While my parents never deprived me of anything, I would never have asked for a luxury that I knew they couldn't afford. I was happy with simple clothes, sneakers, my used Volvo and not eating out a lot. They taught me the value of a dollar. But I also learned that to have some cash, I needed to hustle. I babysat, shoveled driveways, and worked at camp as a CIT at age 14. When I was 16 I worked at Mohawk during the day and Friendly's at night. I busted my ass but loved it. I still am a workaholic. I saw how hard my parents worked and learned that hard work can be and is a good thing.*

Allan also learned generosity. Harry once bought him a "super 8" movie camera when he was still only in fourth grade. Back then, who bought an 8-year-old a movie camera? Allan recognized at some point that Harry would never buy himself a luxury like that, "yet he did it for me." I now know who is responsible for Allan's constant picture posting on Facebook.

Jamie had become a young woman of the newly "liberated" generation. It was not only taken for granted that she would go to college and become a successful professional as well as a wife and mother, it was encouraged. Harry would go up to Skidmore for the special father-daughter weekend called "Happy Pappy" Weekend. It was rare that Jamie got that kind of alone time with him, although it seemed to her that he was more comfortable when they were with other fathers and daughters.

The 1960s was an era when parents started to have enough money to spend on their kids. It was a time to show off the newly found prosperity of a middle-class suburban family. Iris, from a more modern generation, was generous to a fault. She often went overboard on gifts, on donations, on entertaining, on food, and sometimes didn't ask prices.

The two of them were a real contrast. Yet, she was the one who worried about paying the bills, about making things work, on finding ways to pay for sleepaway camp for all of them, Bar Mitzvahs for the boys, cars, private colleges (except for Allan, who still reminds everyone that he went to a New York State public university), weddings, and generous gifts. Harry probably had no clue how much these things cost, and probably knew not to ask because he would have freaked out.

One other way to "show off" was to entertain. Iris did it by cooking up a storm and Harry by putting on his charming face. This dynamic also seems to be typical of the era. As he grew older though, as many do, he talked about himself, and on occasion, seemed to embellish his activities. He had a dry sense of humor, and everyone knew him as the "Pun Master." I remember Harry, Richard, and I often sitting around playing can you top this pun games. When Jamie and I bought our son Ben a book entitled *Puntoons,* and he started drawing his own, Harry was the proudest Poppy.

Harry could use language in a clever way to make his point, and had a great way of slipping in humor to a conversation. He was pretty mild mannered, and gave the best of

himself when engaged in conversation and interaction. Jamie's only regret is that he wasn't more engaged at home, she thinks that it was because he was too tired from his commute and several jobs.

What did entertain Harry? He read the newspaper every day. He knew how to fold the *New York Times* on the train to be mindful of his arm space, and seemed to know what was going on in the world. He loved watching old-time slapstick, like the Three Stooges, and Laurel and Hardy. He liked the weirdness of Jerry Lewis. He would sometimes let out big belly laughs, something he didn't often do. He just seemed to enjoy the shear silliness and sometimes outrageousness of slapstick.

He would enjoy Sunday dinner. In many New York Jewish homes this became ritualistic Sunday at the local Chinese restaurant. When they went out to eat, which was every Sunday, and most often to Tung Sing Chinese Restaurant, Harry had a habit of engaging the waitress/waiter in an extended conversation.

Says Richard,

This would make us a bit crazed because we wanted his attention. We would plead with him to not do this, but invariably he seemed "too interested" in conversing with others. Every Sunday he would ask the waiters at Tung Sing, what flavors of ice cream they had. We knew, and they knew he knew. There were only three, every time. We tried not to giggle when they would say, every week, "Vranella, choc-o-rot, pris-tat-chio."

WATERGATE TRICKLES DOWN TO THE BURNING BRONX

I f you think things are bad now, rejoice. The period between the mid-1970s through the mid-1980s was wildly scary and crazy. Richard Nixon became president. The war in Vietnam ended. Nixon's presidency ended in scandal after he tried to really rig an election. Terrorist acts were global. Israel and the Middle East nations faced hot wars, not just wars of words. Middle East oil-producing countries closed down our oil supplies. Gas prices skyrocketed. Drivers waited for hours on long lines to gas up. Inflation inflated like never before. The Iranians revolted and replaced their long-standing monarchy with a theocracy while holding American hostages for 444 days.

The Equal Rights Amendment for women was passed by Congress but did not get the required number of state legislatures to approve it. *Roe v. Wade* overturned laws against abortion. From fashion to music, everything just seemed to get too out of hand, too big or too flashy. Drugs were rampant. The Bronx burned, literally and figuratively. Hip-hop was born. An actor was elected president. Politics flipped. *Liberal* became a dirty word. And that just scratched the surface.

On Harry's domestic front, Richard graduated from Colgate in 1973 and stayed to get a master's in teaching and to teach in the rural area surrounding the university. Jamie transferred to the University of Pennsylvania after two years at Skidmore. Over the next decade they would each marry and have their first child, and Harry would slide into the role of "Poppy." Allan graduated high school and went off to college in 1979 and left Harry and Iris as empty nesters.

Nineteen seventy-three started off with the official end of the Vietnam War. The Paris Peace Accords were signed in January. The last US troops left two months later. In 1975, the war ended with this ugly scene of Vietnamese allies desperately trying to get on the last American helicopter out of Saigon.

Politically, newly re-inaugurated President Nixon celebrated. Five months later he had reason to worry. The Senate opened its investigation into the 1972 break-in at the Democratic headquarters in the Watergate by the Committee to Re-Elect the President. (CREEP) back when people actually did try to hack (nondigitally) and rig the election. A year later Nixon chose to resign after the House of Representatives impeached him. This was one of the copies of the *New York Times* Harry saved.

http://www.nytimes.com/learning/general/
onthisday/big/0808.html

Vice President Ford took office and promptly pardoned Nixon while Hank Aaron received death threats when his 715th home run broke Babe Ruth's record. Ford apparently wasn't well liked either. The next year he survived two assassination attempts in a seventeen-day span. Jimmy Carter was elected bicentennial president in 1976 and optimistically oversaw the Camp David Peace Accords between Israel and Egypt. That was his high point.

Unfortunately for both him and the United States, the economy bounded from a mid-1970s recession to the worst inflation rates in our history. By 1979, the consumer price index inflation rate hit 14 percent. By 1981, mortgage rates peaked at 17.5 percent for a typical thirty-year mortgage.[90] American car manufacturers were losing out to Japanese and

German cars. Way before the Great Recession of 2008–2009 Chrysler had to be bailed out to avoid bankruptcy.

President Carter, to many a very honest and moral man, didn't help himself with the speech he gave during the summer of 1979 discussing the many economic- and energy-based problems the United States faced. Many thought it one of the greatest presidential speeches of all times; others called it political suicide. The speech was later dubbed the "malaise speech," even though Carter never used that word.

> *The threat is nearly invisible in ordinary ways. It is a crisis of confidence. It is a crisis that strikes at the very heart and soul and spirit of our national will. We can see this crisis in the growing doubt about the meaning of our own lives and in the loss of a unity of purpose for our nation.*[91]

Sounds like us now you think? That was a political nightmare, but compared to what came next, it was a pleasant dream. Nineteen seventy-nine was another year we could have done without. The nuclear plant at Three Mile Island recorded the worst nuclear plant accident in our history. The Shah of Iran fled after being overthrown in December 1978. Searching for a cure for his cancer, he came to the United States almost a year later. When we refused to send him to Iran to stand trial, on November 4, 1979, Islamic militants, led by Ayatollah Khomeini, answered back by storming the US embassy and taking fifty-two American hostages for 444 days. Things got even worse with a failed rescue attempt in the spring of 1980.

Donald Trump would actually have been factually correct calling that era a mess.

Things in 1980 didn't improve. Oh, yes. Sandra Day O'Connor did become the first woman on the Supreme Court, but the United States boycotted the Summer Olympics to protest the Soviet invasion of Afghanistan. Yes, that Afghanistan. A real volcano, Mount St. Helens, erupted in the state of Washington. John Lennon was assassinated.

Then came Reagan, and another assassination attempt. He cut the top income tax rate from 70 percent to 50 percent, and thus gave teeth to his supply side, Reagonomic, trickle-down, and voodoo economic ideas. Almost 250 US Marines were killed in a terrorist bombing in Lebanon.

We invaded Grenada. What? We invaded a city in Spain? No. Actually, we attacked a tiny island in the Caribbean. Why invade this little island of 100,000 souls? Ostensibly it was because US citizens attended the medical school there, but the reality was that it was to overthrow a newly established pro-communist regime.

Finally, in retaliation for the 1980 boycott of the Summer Olympics in Moscow, the Soviet Union and its allies boycotted the 1984 Olympics in Los Angeles. Can we all grow up now please? After just witnessing the 2016 presidential election and the Trump administration, I guess not.

On the other hand, technology and communication continued to change our lives forever. Skylab and the Space Shuttle *Columbia* were launched, rekindling our interest in space exploration, but this was to be a consumer revolution. HBO began in 1975. Bill Gates launched Microsoft. Sony's Betamax allowed for commercial home video, the first home video game system, Atari, was released, and the Commodore PET became the first home personal computer. CNN became the first twenty-four-hour cable news network. MTV became the first twenty-four-hour cable music network. Chrysler began to sell mini-vans. Fox Broadcasting Company opened its doors in 1986. Automation began to slowly replace workers in many of our major manufacturing industries, invisibly creating a jobs problem that the next generations had to face. It was the beginning of a revolution we so strongly feel the effects of today.

#Ohhowefeelthoseeffectstoday.

How far had we come regarding civil rights and economic equity, after the promises of the 1960s? If there was one place in the United States that showed how little had changed, it was the burning down of my little neck of the woods, the Bronx, New York. Not only was I raised in the Bronx, but Jamie and I also lived there for the first ten years of our marriage. What went on concerned us and Jamie's parents who only knew what they read or saw on TV. Was it fake news? Some was.

The Bronx, and several other New York City neighborhoods represented the urban decay, decline, and debacle that came to urban areas all across the nation. The South Bronx, including neighborhoods where I had grown up, had become an area of incredible institutional poverty.

The South Bronx (along with Brooklyn's Brownsville, Bushwick, and Bedford-Stuyvesant neighborhoods) was, in fact, burning. Seven different census tracts in the Bronx lost more than 97 percent of their buildings to fire and abandonment between 1970 and 1980. Forty-four census tracts (out of 289 in the borough) lost more than 50 percent. In one night in July 1977, 400 fires were reported. Twenty percent of the population left the borough.[92]

The famous photograph of Jimmy Carter standing in a lot on Charlotte Street shows the burnt-out shell of the building in which my grandmother lived decades before. From 1955 to 1963 I lived just a few blocks away.

https://www.nytsyn.com/archives/photos/751656.html

During this period, the NYPD's 41st Precinct Station House on Simpson Street be-
came known as "Fort Apache, The Bronx" as it struggled to deal with the overwhelm-
ing surge of violent crime, which for the entirety of the 1970s (and part of the early
1980s) made South Bronx the murder, rape, robbery, aggravated assault and arson
capitals of America. By 1980, the 41st was renamed "The Little House on the Prai-
rie", as fully 2/3 of the 94,000 residents originally served by the precinct had fled, leav-
ing the fortified station house as one of the few structures in the neighborhood (and
the sole building on Simpson Street) that had not been abandoned or burnt out."[93]

How does this relate to Harry? His daughter lived in the Bronx, a mere three miles north
of the fire zone. Jamie and I married in November 1974. Iris had actually pointed me out
to Jamie when we all worked at Mohawk Day Camp. At some point in their lives every
Greissman except Harry worked at that local camp.

Iris liked me and was happy for Jamie to get settled so young, as she had. Harry
apparently also gave his approval after playing tennis with me and then reporting that
based on what he saw in the locker room, I had "all the right equipment." The marriage
was therefore blessed. I hadn't realized that when I asked him for his permission, I had to
pass a physical.

Harry and Iris wanted the best for their kids, and their soon to be second grandchild.

Harry had been a terrific athlete, and was in great shape, but over the years as had
many men his age and from the weekend warrior generation developed a paunch for which
he took much ridicule from the family. As Jamie came closer and closer to giving birth, we
all noticed an interesting family resemblance and teased him to no end about it.

The Family Estate

Although the nice Jewish neighborhood Jamie and I lived in was a fair distance from the flames of the South Bronx, on the edge of more tony Riverdale, Harry and Iris were never really happy that Jamie Beth Beautiful Greissman Greene was living there, in *The Bronx Is Burning* Bronx. But there we stayed for ten years because Jamie was commuting to Long Island to get her master's at Columbia then her doctorate at Hofstra University, and I was teaching in the southeast Bronx. That was until we were about to have a child.

I'm not sure whose idea it was—probably Iris's—but the discussion about us buying their house came up as they became more and more worried about where we lived, and we were beginning to look for houses in the suburbs of Westchester County. We had looked around at a few places that were out of our price range. Jamie had just finished getting her doctorate in psychology and had just started working. The problem was that anything we could afford we really didn't want. Iris reasoned that the house was getting too difficult for them to manage, and that since Harry was still working (and scarily driving to Connecticut), a move to a condo in northern Westchester County would be good for them, as well as for Jamie and me.

Furthermore, if we bought the house, they could avoid the cleaning out process, which they both avoided for good reasons. HIS garage and HIS basement were loaded with stuff. Loaded? There was barely a walking aisle with each side piled head high with who knows what. "I am not a hoarder, I am a collector," he would say. The Collyer brothers may have been his idols. Let's just say he had trouble throwing stuff out. Harry would not part with things. Iris wanted to avoid the inevitable arguments that would ensue. So, they both reasoned that we should buy the house, AS IS, and we would have to deal with the cleanup.

Allan says,

If the TV show, Hoarders, existed back in the 70s, Dad would have been a star. Our garage was one big storage (dumping) area, with lots of his old books, magazines [including Playboys] and junk. He would try to hide his cigarettes there. I would find them and destroy them.

171

I have to say that buying the Greissman "Estate" was not what I wanted. I had been visiting their house in Ardsley for over ten years and thought (still do) the town abysmally ugly, especially compared with other Westchester County towns. It was a series of strip malls along business route 9A and had no redeeming value for me. I was not a fan of the suburbs. I thought it a sample of ticky tacky suburban houses all built in a row.

It reminded me of the song "Little Boxes" by Malvina Reynolds. I didn't want that to be us.

> *Little boxes on the hillside,*
> *Little boxes made of ticky tacky,*
> *Little boxes on the hillside,*
> *Little boxes all the same.*
> *There's a green one and a pink one*
> *And a blue one and a yellow one,*
> *And they're all made out of ticky tacky*
> *And they all look just the same.*
> *And the people in the houses*
> *All went to the university,*
> *Where they were put in boxes*
> *And they came out all the same,*
>
> *And there's doctors and lawyers,*
> *And business executives,*
> *And they're all made out of ticky tacky*
> *And they all look just the same.*
>
> *And they all play on the golf course*
> *And drink their martinis dry,*
> *And they all have pretty children*
> *And the children go to school,*
> *And the children go to summer camp*
> *And then to the university,*
> *Where they are put in boxes*
> *And they come out all the same.*
>
> *And the boys go into business*
> *And marry and raise a family*
> *In boxes made of ticky tacky*
> *And they all look just the same.*
> *There's a green one and a pink one*
> *And a blue one and a yellow one,*
> *And they're all made out of ticky tacky*
> *And they all look just the same.*

But Jamie loved the house. She had grown up there. She remembered the warmth, the family, and the experiences she shared with Harry, Iris, Richard, and Allan.

So, we bought it. But before we did, we suggested to them that they replace the drafty front bay window and the old boiler, two energy sucks. Harry, surprisingly, agreed to spend his money on those improvements, fully knowing we would buy it soon. They also gave the house to us for a price we could afford and lost a lot of money on the deal as a result. Harry was, in that way, very generous to us both.

Once we moved in, they enjoyed coming over and seeing the changes we made. Little by little, particularly after we put on an addition just as our second child, Ben, was born in 1990 (literally—they finished when Jamie went into labor!), they would claim they wanted the house back from us! They loved that we were raising our kids in their family homestead. Harry enjoyed finding his old places of refuge. His only frustration was in going into our clean garage, and remarking that we had thrown out some "precious" tools or items. He would wince, because these items were invariably so "valuable." I secretly thought he was proud that we could accomplish that.

They bought a two-bedroom condominium in Jefferson Village, Yorktown Heights, with its own garage for Harry to put his remaining "stuff." In retrospect, had he not kept some of what we all called junk, at 10 Kenneth or at the new condo, there would not be the wealth of information available to write this book. Also in retrospect, I have realized that what he saved was his life. It was not only memories, but also the evidence of his achievements, intellect, and of soaring. No wonder he was so protective of it all. It was his legacy.

THE NEXT GENERATION

Meanwhile in rural upstate New York, Richard was teaching and becoming a rare Colgate student who successfully became a popular local guy. He lived in Hamilton, New York, where he was a volunteer fireman while he taught social studies at nearby Sherbrook Earlville High School.

Both Iris and Harry were proud of his accomplishments in his professional life, but it was clear that Iris mother was disappointed that he was not making more money.

> *It was a nuanced disappointment in that the conversations always began with how pleased she was and how she marveled at my talents, in particular my ability to communicate with word and pen—and my ability to communicate with other people. But that was always the prologue to the disappointment: with those talents why weren't you doing more, where "more" meant having a job with greater status and financial return.*

Looking back, it was very clear that Iris was afraid that Richard, so much like Harry in all those respects, would turn out like Harry, to her a disappointment financially and professionally.

Harry, on the other hand, was always keen to know the details of Richard's work, especially when it involved complex academic and intellectual problems or brought him into contact with notable people. This was their bond. They shared these attributes. In Richard, Harry saw the best parts of him, and that forged a special bond. He could not share any of that with Iris, Jamie, or Allan. He could with me, and I think that pleased him about Jamie's choice, other than my physical attributes.

In particular, he loved the fact that Richard was an innovative and creative teacher. Harry, unlike Iris, saw Richard's calling to teach a blessing, and perhaps felt, jealously wished, that teaching and not advertising had become his own vocation. He was at least

Thoroughly professional-looking Harry in a thoughtful moment with his niece Marnie.

pleased to know that Richard had followed in his footsteps, even though his work as a volunteer fireman and elected village trustee was alien to him. Harry loved Richard's choices, his new wife included, except for geographic location. On the other hand, Iris was clearly thinking out loud "What kind of work is that for a nice Jewish boy?"

My daughter Lindsay was born a few months after we moved in to 10 Kenneth. She was not his first grandchild. Richard had already married (more to come on this). He and his wife Randolph decided to work as teachers in Zimbabwe (formerly the British colony of Rhodesia) shortly after it gained its independence. Okay, let's just say that Richard's decision to travel to and work in a newly born, revolutionary, African nation did not go over well at 10 Kenneth, especially with Iris.

Harry and Iris were extremely nervous, as this was, to them, a dangerous place to be, even worse than the Bronx. While there, Richard and Randolph had a daughter and named her Rudo, which is a Shona (one of the native tongues in Zimbabwe) word for love. This pissed off Harry and Iris no end. Why is a nice Jewish boy naming his child using an African tongue, and not following Jewish tradition of naming children after family members who have passed away, usually great grandparents? And why is a nice Jewish boy with so much going for him then moving his family to Lexington, Kentucky, in March 1984, after living in rural upstate New York, and rural Zimbabwe?

The answer was twofold. First, Richard landed a job as assistant headmaster at the Lexington school in Lexington. The second? Richard's new wife, Randolph Hollingsworth, was from a well-placed, long-standing, Episcopalian, Lexington family. In fact, her first name, Randolph is a tribute to the Virginia Randolphs of the Revolutionary age ancestry. Randolph very much wanted to keep her name after marriage, and did. That too, did not go over well. Then they had Rudo. Both Harry and Iris had wanted her to be named after Iris's sister Ruth. At least Rudo started with an "R."

Then things got even more interesting. Would Rudo be Rudo Hollingsworth-Greissman? Can you imagine fitting that last name on the back of any team uniform? Would she be Rudo Hollingsworth? Rudo Greissman? Richard and Randolph came up with a novel solution to the name game that they thought would easily solve the problem. Rudo and any future offspring would have their own combined last name—"Greissworth." That did not go over well either.

Harry and Iris were both really angry at the loss of the passing down of the family name. Harry also misconstrued it to believe that Richard was also changing his last name to Greissworth. It was probably a good thing that the Hollingsworth, Greissman, Greissworth family lived almost 750 miles away. Time and distance eventually tempered things, or at least Harry didn't really say much about it. I don't think Iris ever got over it.

Lindsay, about a year and a half younger than Rudo, was home. Literally. She was being raised at 10 Kenneth and was only about a half-hour drive from the condo and at least she had a normal name.

When Richard finally returned with Rudo, when she was not yet a year old, and came to New York to have everyone meet her, Harry's joy was so evident, his smile said it all. Problem solved.

TOWARD THE
TWENTY-FIRST
CENTURY

Aside from being Harry's "Poppy" years, the 1980s and 1990s were, except for a brief four years, will be remembered as the Reagan-Clinton years, dominated by two charismatic "Teflonic" presidential characters.

http://www.washingtontimes.com/topics/ronald-reagan/

http://reuther.wayne.edu/node/9146

Prior to his election, Ronald Reagan was a former actor turned governor of California. Bill Clinton was an Oxford scholar turned youngest governor in American history, although in Arkansas. Reagan was the oldest president, 69, when elected, and Clinton the third youngest. Reagan was in Harry's generation, Bill in ours.

Harry, never really let on much about his politics, but he was a fiscally conservative Roosevelt Democrat. He was far more interested in his work, his family, and his tennis.

Richard and I disliked Reagan and everything he stood for. He was the antithesis of our 1960s norms and values. He worried us. But he did lead the way to ending the Cold War with a slowly collapsing Soviet regime. On a visit to Berlin in 1987 he demanded then Soviet Premier Mikhail Gorbachev to, "Tear down this wall" (the Berlin Wall). He negotiated a treaty with Gorbachev that was another break in the nuclear arms race. However, he bombed Libya, the Iran-Contra scandal unfolded, Pan Am Flight 103 was bombed over Scotland, and we shot down an Iranian Airliner. Oops! That wall finally did come down in 1989, when President George H. W. (not to be confused with his son George Dubya) was elected president and he, with Soviet Premier Gorbachev released statements indicating that the Cold War between their nations may be coming to an end.

On the other hand, domestically, trickle-down economics trickled up as income inequity rose, more US industries moved overseas or workers were replaced even more with automated machines, more jobs were lost, and more unions were busted. *Greed*-motivated Wall Street *Barbarians at the Gate* bought and destroyed businesses in hostile takeovers. Regulations of many industries just disappeared. The Dow Jones Industrial Average dropped almost 25 percent in one day in 1987. The *Exxon Valdez* spilled millions of tons of crude oil on the Alaska coastline. Harry retired.

The oil spill was successfully cleaned up, but nature struck during the last half of the 1980s as well. Hurricane Hugo left $7 billion worth of damage, and an earthquake in the middle of a World Series game devastated San Francisco.

Since we, as Americans, often tend to end decades when there is a presidential election, which happens more often than not, these 1980s under Bush 1 lasted until 1992. The pre-Clinton 1990s included a war in Iraq, setting the stage for a twenty-first century filled with never-ending wars there. They also included a domestic war in Los Angeles. After the videotaped beating of black motorist Rodney King was aired, riots erupted in "La La Land" resulting in over fifty deaths and about $1 billion in damages.

However, the most devastating event during George H. W.'s reign was a hurricane, this one named Andrew, that slammed Florida, just south of Miami leaving over $26 billion in damages and killing sixty-five people. It was the most destructive storm ever to hit the United States. Son, George W., would have to face the results of Katrina, the even more destructive storm in the Gulf Coast thirteen years later. Bush luck?

Harry did not survive to see the twenty-first century. He passed away in December 1997. But he lived through most of the 1990s and experienced the "Clinton Years." Who was Bill Clinton? To many he was a bright young governor who would move the country forward with new ideas. To others he was a threatening throwback to Liberalism. To Liberals he was a not so liberal "centrist." To them his "Third Way" thinking was too close to more conservative and business ideas. To many he was simply a "triangulator" with his sole purpose being to get credit for passing legislation, regardless of ideology.

To Doonesbury cartoonist, Garry Trudeau, he was all three as in this image regarding the universal health care being pushed by his wife Hillary. Trudeau saw Clinton as a waffle following the polls and not principle. Harry was skeptical, seeing a possible New Deal liberal, yet not.

Whether a result of President Clinton or not, the 1990s was a far greater success for most Americans than we had seen in decades. Many boomers like to think that it is the results of the maturing of their generation. Among the accomplishments of the Clinton administration was the longest economic expansion in American history. Americans gained 22 million new jobs, the highest home owner rate ever, the lowest unemployment rate in thirty years, the lowest crime rate in over twenty-five years, the lowest poverty rate in twenty years, the lowest teen birth rate in sixty years, and the lowest infant mortality rate in our history. In addition, the largest budget deficit in our history became the largest surplus in our history, while at the same time the tax burden dropped to its lowest level since 1966. Whew. That was a lot of good stuff for a waffle to be responsible for.

However, things were not all rosy. We suffered through both man-made and natural disasters. We seem to forget that terror existed before September 11, 2001. First a truck bomb exploded in the parking garage under the World Trade Center, killing six and injuring thousands in 1993. During that same year the FBI siege of the Branch Davidian cult in Waco, Texas, ended the lives of seventy-six men women and children. Two years later, the Oklahoma City bombing of the federal building by Timothy McVeigh and Terry Nichols was the worst domestic terrorist incident in US history. It killed 168 people and wounded approximately 800.

Nineteen ninety-five brought us the infamous OJ Simpson trial that split the nation racially when he was acquitted of murdering his ex-wife, Nicole Brown Simpson, and Ronald Goldman. There was no letup in 1996 either. A TWA jet blew up right after taking off from New York's Kennedy Airport killing all 230 passengers and crew. Nineteen US servicemen were killed in a Saudi housing complex, and finally the Centennial Olympic park in Atlanta, Georgia, was bombed during the Summer Olympics. Harry passed away before the horror of the school shooting at Columbine and the Egypt Air disaster killing 217 in 1999.

Naturally, things didn't go well during the mid-1990s either. Another "Blizzard of the Century" hit the east coast causing $6 billion in damages. Nature ravaged the Midwest as well that year with the flooding of both the Mississippi and Missouri Rivers causing three times as much damage. Los Angeles suffered through the Northridge earthquake that killed 72, injured approximately 9,000, and cost about $20 billion in damages.

The 1990s also included impeachment charges of a seated president for only the third time in our history. The crimes? Sexual misconduct. One might say that was both a man-made and natural disaster. Whew, and then we were ready for the coming of the new century. The coming of the new century was not without more fears. Wow. The twenty-first century. Oh no, Y2K, the millennium bug. Were our computers going to transfer over to everything starting with 20, not 19? Would all systems shut down?

No, but maybe our ability to be rational did. This was way before fake news, Facebook, Twitter, and other social media has magnified the events we face now so greatly that we think the world is coming to an end. As we look back, however, at those events of the twentieth century Harry and his generation endured, we need to "check" ourselves. History speaks volumes.

To Florida
and Beyond

When Harry and Iris sold us 10 Kenneth, they were doing what so many of their friends and others of their generation did. First, they downsized to a condo in Yorktown Heights, New York. Then, they became "snowbirds," living half the year in New York and wintering in Florida. Finally, they followed the fold and moved year-round to Florida.

Downsizing became a common suburbanite trait that developed during the latter part of the twentieth century. After their children left them, Greatest Generation and baby boomer empty nesters in the New York area and near other cities moved into a newly growing segment of housing called condominiums, or as my Uncle Irving used to call them "cockaminions." To many historians the boom in condominium development, especially in places with warm weather climates, was a direct result of Harry's Greatest Generation passing through this time of their life.

Cooperatives existed in the United States since the end of World War I and had grown significantly in Florida from the late 1950s and 1960s, leading to the large exodus of retiring Northeasterners that included a huge number of New York Jews. The difference between a cooperative and condominium is simple. When you "buy" an apartment that is in a co-op building you are really only buying shares of the private corporation that owns the building. Condominiums are privately owned.

Retirement to warm weather areas beckoned and real estate developers saw an opportunity to make money. Their lobbyists got Congress to amend FHA rules to allow condo financing, and the concept of owning an apartment went mainstream. All across the United States the Greatest Generation and the baby boomers sold their single family dwellings and moved either to a "condo" or townhouse near where they lived and worked, or a "cockaminion" in Florida or Arizona when they retired. They became options in the north as well.

181

Harry enjoyed the condo life. It was easier. There were no outside chores. After all he was now approaching 70 years of age. Shit, so am I, and I just downsized to a "cockaminion." Allan and Richard were gone and there was no one to mow that steep lawn or shovel that long steep driveway without having to pay someone. Now I don't either.

Although he missed his screened-in porch where he could have a smoke, He and Iris were even closer to Lou and Anita's house in Mahopac. Harry's relationship with Lou was special. Lou was an older brother, successful and knowledgeable about many things. The brothers loved to sit on Lou's patio, overlooking Lake Mahopac, and talk about whatever came to their minds. Harry would smoke his pipe, or a cigar, or maybe even a hidden cigarette. They would talk, even get a bit loud at times, laugh, and had a genuine affection and deep bond for one another. Harry appreciated Lou's mind. Lou also appreciated Harry's mind, and that was something Harry sorely needed.

Years before Lou had a serious stroke that left him with a tracheal tube and months of rehab. Whereas Harry seemed rarely patient at home, he was extremely patient and attentive to Lou who had to relearn talking, walking, etc. Although his brilliant mind remained intact, his speech was somewhat difficult to understand, but Harry and Lou talked as though there was never any difficulty and Lou seemed comfortable with the absence of judgment.

Harry and Iris finally decided to move to Florida full time. Richard came to Yorktown to help them pack. After taking box loads of books to the local library, cartons of clothes and other charitable goods to local charity outlets, he started to tackle the job of packing up the more precious items in the house—such as a grandfather clock, glass figurines, and other artwork. They had planned to ship those things, but Richard didn't want them to worry about the breakage, so he took it to a local UPS to get it professionally boxed up.

It was expensive but I felt I had to defend the decision to Iris by having economized elsewhere and satisfied myself that they would arrive intact. Harry had been hovering in the background. He asked who paid for it. When he found out Iris had given me their credit card he was furious. This was a pattern often revisited a number of times over our adult lives together where I would make a decision or be complicit in a decision Iris made and he would explode because he felt I had been profligate in my spending of their money.

That left Allan, remember Allan? After graduating from SUNY Albany, Allan lived with us at 10 Kenneth. It is a good thing we cleared out that basement, because it became Allan's room. He took a year off to finish courses so he could apply to medical school. Off he went to Richmond to the Medical College of Virginia.

Jamie recalled an incident at Allan's medical school graduation that was pure Harry.

We were all in Richmond for Allan's graduation. We had breakfast at the hotel and then got into two or three cars to go. When we got to the ceremony, we realized Dad was not in any of the cars. Richard [of course] went back to the hotel to find him. He had quietly gone off to his room and we all thought he was in one of the other cars.

Maybe he had stopped off to chat with someone.

After his four years at medical school In Richmond, Virginia, Allan returned to New York for his residency and married. He lived for a while in Bayside, Queens, and recalls another example of Harry's "Depression mentality,"

> *He and mom came to visit us in Bayside, Queens, during my residency. We went out to dinner. He asked the waitress the price of the rainbow trout dinner special. When he heard the price, he quickly switched his order to pancakes. I was mortified, embarrassed. But that was Dad. Frugal and a bit tight. [Allan wonders, today]* "Maybe that's why I'm to the other extreme?"

As Harry and his grandchildren grew older he couldn't stop himself from storytelling, reading, and celebrating birthdays with his young ones. His bonds with them, like with Lou, were boundless. Maybe he felt they appreciated him. The only problem was the increased separation as Harry and Iris snowbirded, then moved permanently to Florida.

Even in this new place, he loved his routine. He played tennis each day early enough so the grueling heat and humidity didn't sap all of his energy. He showered for an hour, or what seemed like it because it took him forever to come out. He ate lunch, usually on the screened-in terrace where he could also smoke his pipe and read his newspapers. That usually led to a nap, either because the news was boring him or it was just part of the routine. Had much really changed? At least he was relaxed. He still seemed most relaxed while alone.

Jamie thinks he seemed happy there. But was he, away from his children and his grandchildren most of the time? He and Iris would go to social activities, but once they moved there for good, Allan believes they started to grow apart.

Iris tried to keep busy renting apartments, playing bridge, and being social, but there were signs of a developing dementia. Although it was not too bad, Harry had very little patience for her. She and Allan could not put up with his being so ornery.

Iris spent a lot of time at Allan's house in nearby Weston helping with granddaughter Sammy and grandson Jordan, who were only 6 and 3 when Harry died. Harry didn't come a lot. Allan thinks this is when he started to grow distant form Harry. He felt his kids did not have a strong relationship with him like they did with Dudley, their other grandfather. Jamie and I never got that impression when he was with Lindsay, or Ben, nor did Richard feel that way when he was with Rudo and Richard's younger daughter Ellie. But then again, we rarely saw him once they moved to Florida.

Allan and Harry would watch sports and talk, but "he just wasn't the same." When he could no longer play tennis he clearly was just not the same mentally or physically. Harry never was an emotionally outgoing or "kid friendly" guy. Allan admits,

> *Sadly I am embarrassed to say that I did not enjoy my time with Dad as much. I still punish myself with the memories of not spending more time with him.*

Lindsay, who was in New York, has few memories of him. Ben barely remembers some events. Richard's youngest daughter Ellie in Kentucky, and Allan's youngest child Jordan, do not remember him at all. They were 13, 7, 6, and 2 when he died.

Yet, oldest grandchild Rudo, who was 15 when he passed away and clearly inherited Harry's way with words, recalls,

Pushing back to the farthest limits of my memories I remember another house, before they moved to the apartment. I remember a room with a Lazy-Boy type chair and how it smelled of pipe tobacco. I remember on very seldom occasions SEEING him pack his pipe and catching a waft of his pungent smoke. To this day I LOATHE the smell of cigars but LOVE the smell of pipe tobacco. I'm assuming this is because I associate pipes with my beloved Poppy.

My various memories of Poppy are like snapshots, no longer than the attention span of a 5-year-old or so. All of them are filled with a gentle benevolence. The quietness of a man full of many thoughts but at ease with himself and his surrounding so not pressured to expand on many of them. I remember his gaze, his kind blue eyes resting on me. Once I was looking at myself in the mirrored wall that made up part of the dining room at their Ft. Lauderdale apartment. I must have had a worried look because he spoke up. "You are so beautiful Rudo," he said. "Just look at that wonderful face." Instantly I was at ease.

Once we were alone in the car together. I remember it was at an airport. I had Michael Crichton's novel Jurassic Park in my hands. He asked if I was enjoying the book and when I replied yes he pushed further. "What have you learned so far? You know Crichton pays great attention to detail and research." I remember discussing chaos theory with him, in my elementary level way, and how he just listened and seemed to be impressed with me. Knowing now just how intelligent he was, I am amazed at his control to have just listened to his young granddaughter and not have needed to impress upon me what HE KNEW, but rather allow me to flesh out my own understanding.

I remember being vaguely worried about him when I asked what the funny machine was by his bed. Someone explained to me it was to help him breathe at night. I remember running to him, hugging his bulbous generous belly. I remember his embrace, so strong and protective. I wish I could quote him exactly, but that has never been a skill of mine. I just remember being awed at his way with words. As if he were painting, as if he had lovingly chosen JUST THE RIGHT words for that thought. He was succinct, but colorful. This was something I just remember feeling, I remember relishing anything he'd say, as he was prone to talking.

His joy at having his grandchildren near him was palpable. That's what made him such a wonderful grandfather ... we could FEEL his delight in our presence, and that authenticity came with few but precious encouraging observations. He was so observant, and encouraged my gifts in such a way that I felt he saw a wonderful potential.

This was no blind support; he really took the time to qualify what he was impressed by. He was the most thoughtful man in my young life aside from his son, my father. They are so similar, and my dad really shares that thoughtful tenderness.

Blowing out a birthday ice cream dish with Rudo

With my mom, me, Jamie, and Iris.
With Allan.

Every one of us comes into this world part of a family, and ultimately we leave it that way. Harry's journey through life began as a son and brother. He became uncle, husband, "pop," Harry-in-law, and finally "Poppy."

After retirement took his work away, after he was unable to write that promised novel or great book about advertising, after his legs no longer allowed him to play tennis the way he used to, and after he saw the mental deterioration of his beloved Iris start to take her away from him, his new vocation became "Poppy."

Six months before he passed away, my daughter Lindsay was Bat Mitzvah. He cut and blessed the challah. He posed. And he danced his last dance with his daughter, Jamie Beth Beautiful. Six months later he was no longer with us.

Rudo expands,

He loved to drink Scotch. I remember one time when I was really little, maybe 4 or 5. He had been drinking something that I figured was apple juice. He had gotten up from his chair and left the drink on the table. I remember wanting to be just like Poppy, so I sat in his chair and took a sip of his "apple juice," only to immediately spit out the drink upon realizing it was definitively NOT apple juice.

Poppy would often sit in his cozy chair in his bedroom/balcony in Florida, reading the newspaper and smoking his pipe. There was something very familiar and comforting about that pipe smell, its scent almost fruity and sweet. Any time I smell a pipe, I am immediately reminded of my sweet, gentle Poppy.

Lindsay adds,

Poppy was an avid tennis enthusiast. Playing tennis with Poppy was one of my favorite things to do when we visited my grandparents in Florida. I remember watching him in his tennis whites, round belly protruding over his thin, muscular legs, wondering how he didn't topple over! His face lit up on the tennis court, especially when he played with my mom, who certainly inherited his tennis DNA.

Poppy was an extremely intelligent, loyal, man who didn't talk all the time, but when he did, he made me feel extremely special and loved. He loved his family, especially my mom, and I felt proud to be his granddaughter.

Oh also, he wasn't allowed to drive because he would always get lost/was a terrible driver.

Everyone remembers that.

THIS IS THE END

Harry played tennis until about six months before he died. Even at his age he was a superior player. His legs simply gave out. No one knows much about how death might be brought on sooner with the loss of desire or ability to do the things you love. We think it drained part of his soul. So maybe what followed in six months was his body reacting to that loss.

Allan tells these stories.

On August 31, 1997, the Jets played an away game at Miami. Perhaps because of my memories of him taking me to the '69 Mets World Series game, I took dad to the game at Dolphins Stadium. It had to be 100 degrees. It was hard for him to walk by this time. We parked and Dad somehow managed to walk all the way into the stadium and to our seats. He sweated up a storm and I was convinced he was going to have a stroke. The seats were in the seventh row. I remember him slowly walking up all the steps to get to the bathroom.

Dad enjoyed the Jets game. I got him a hot dog, bag of peanuts, and a soda. He really wasn't a beer guy. He was happy as a pig in a poke and I was too. It's ironic to me that my son Jordan, who I was blessed to be able to take to any sporting event he wanted, never was into sports. He would go, to be with me, but never really enjoyed it.

Ronnie [his ex-wife] and I would go to Disney a lot, take first Sammy then Jordan too. Sometime Mom would go up with us. It was fun having her. Dad rarely went, again due to the walking. I remember him once getting very insulted and angry with us when we suggested that we get a wheelchair to make it easier for him to get around. My father was too proud/stubborn to admit he needed a wheelchair.

Dad was in decent health despite being overweight. He wasn't on a lot of meds and never got sick. But in his last years he just wasn't happy. He slept a lot and I think his snoring (obstructive sleep apnea) was so severe that he just never got a good night's sleep.

He was hospitalized for an infection in his leg, yet was recovering and expecting to be released from the hospital when he had a heart attack. Allan was able to be there because he lived nearby.

> *Back then I worked at a hospital, Plantation General. If I was on call, I would get calls at night from them. Dad was admitted for a routine foot infection. He was getting IV antibiotics. I went to visit him late one afternoon. I stopped at the doctor's lounge to get us both an ice cream. His eyes lit up when I showed up with the treat. We watched TV together and I left that evening.*
>
> *Then the phone rang around 4 am. I knew something was wrong. I wasn't on call, why would they be calling me. It was Chris. He was an adult ER doctor there I knew very well. He said, "Allan, your father just had a heart attack. He is in the ICU, on a ventilator. Come in soon."*
>
> *When I got there, there was Dad. A breathing tube was down his throat. Wires and tubes were everywhere. They said he had a massive heart attack and it was not likely he would recover. Mom was there, but her mind wasn't sharp. Rich and Jamie were at home. We spoke. We all knew that Dad would never want to live hooked up to a machine. If he couldn't get up to go to the porch and read the paper, then life wasn't worth living. We signed a Do Not Resuscitate form (a DNR). It was the hardest decision of my life. Rich and Jamie came to see him. Jamie returned home. One or two nights later, Richard left the hospital after seeing Dad. Quietly and peacefully, Dad died a few hours later.*

Richard and Jamie had to watch from afar and try to figure out whether or when to fly down to see him. They went down to see him, Jamie missing our son Ben's 7th birthday party. When she saw him, she was horrified. Aware, trying to talk while tubed and hooked up to a ventilator that prevented him from doing so, his frustration was clear. Communication was his life's blood, and that was taken away. Told that he would recover, Jamie felt relieved enough that she went back home, planning to go back during Christmas vacation, which was only three days away. He never made it. His first heart attack had been December 12, Ben's birthday. He had another heart attack five days later and passed away on December 18, 1997. He was 82.

His three kids felt it was a blessing because if he were disabled or unable to talk, walk, and communicate, he would have been very unhappy. He died just at a time Richard and Jamie were bringing their families down to Florida for Christmas break. Maybe he tried to keep it convenient for their schedules. He never wanted to interfere with their work and lives.

> *When Dad died, it took me years to get over his death. During his last years I didn't see him as much. He was crotchety and not fun to be with. I was embarrassed at times to be with him. To this day I still have tremendous guilt for not spending more time with him ... and then he died. I was with a psychologist for a long time trying to get over that.*

He was just a humble, simple lifestyle guy who just loved the simple pleasure ... tennis, the New York Times, a good big bowl of ice cream. A Depression era man who wasn't flashy or outgoing, he was a quiet guy content on being a family man. He lived a very simple but complete life. He never had fancy stuff in the house. Sure, he bought a color TV when they first came out, but he drove an American Motors "Green Hornet." He didn't travel a lot, gamble, or live a flashy life. But he lived a life that many others wished they could. The people he met and worked with admired his flair for international marketing and public relations. People came to him for his wisdom and thoughts as an orator, writer and thinker.

By the way, Mom and Dad ... When you read the book, you should know something. When we went to Hamilton for Richard's graduation from Colgate. Remember that we shared that hotel room with you two in one bed, and me in the other? You thought I was sleeping. I wasn't, but pretended to. Dad wanted to fool around with Mom. You did ... scarred me for life ... my parents having sex in the bed next to me."

—*Allan*

One of the things about Uncle Harry was his ability to aggrandize and embellish a tale to fit what he wanted it to be or maybe that was what he really saw, I don't know. Some would say he exaggerated. I remember the last time I saw him we were going to visit Allan in his new home in Florida. On the way there Uncle Harry went on about Allan's "mansion." Now don't get me wrong, it was a beautiful home and a father could not of been prouder of a son than Harry but a mansion was a stretch.

—*Susan*

He had a great way of listening to others, of absorbing what they were saying and in making connections. I always thought that my interest in being a psychologist came from my outgoing social skills and loving making connections, which was so much my mother's way. But in thinking about what I love in doing my work, it is my father's legacy of listening to another, absorbing their thoughts and ideas, and in helping make connections.

He was an enormously smart and talented man, who on the one hand gave so much to others in his quiet gentler manner. My friends always found him kind, interested in them, and engaging. He was a true Renaissance man.

—*Jamie*

When I was 13 or so I attended a leadership training camp in Kentucky. One of the exercises involved an empty chair with a circle of us gathered around it. The facilitator said we would all take turns addressing the chair, imagining whomever we liked to be sitting in it. It was a deeply moving session for all involved, and my turn left an indelible impact on me. I remember the room being so quiet, and all the lights had been turned off so the window far off at the end of the large conference room was the only source of light. All eyes on me, I began by explaining to the group I was choosing to imagine my Grandpa Harry in the chair, who had passed away.

I started awkwardly, thanking him for his devotion to being an attentive grandparent. I recounted the long phone calls where I'd play my most recent piano piece I was learning, or I'd read aloud an essay I was working on for school. As I began to paint the portrait of his love the rest of the room melted away. The empty red chair disappeared and all I felt were warm tears down my cheeks. I lamented at his passing, wished he were still available for a chat. I thanked him for his unconditional love, for the times we could just sit together in silence.

I remember saying "You changed my life Poppy, you made me feel appreciated and understood as a young woman and an intellect. Your love gave me confidence, and you're always with me." I think from that time on I've carried him with me, or should I say his presence could always be felt by me. I think of him as my patron saint.

—Rudo

Rudo and Iam, who would have
been his first great grandson.

He could indeed make words sing.

RELAX

We are all ordinary people living in our own ordinary times. As my friend Harris says, "We all think our times are the most extraordinary 'evvvvverrrr.'" However bad things might seem as we read this today, they are really rather historically ordinary. Our times do not compare with the extraordinary times Harry's generation faced.

Yes, we face economic inequality and loss of jobs, but the unemployment rate is under 5 percent, not hovering at 25 percent as it was in the Great Depression. Yes, we face racial issues but de jure segregation is pretty much gone. Black Lives Matters would have had a far more difficult task then, when lynching was rampant and whole parts of cities like Tulsa were destroyed by whites. Broken health care system? There was none to break then. Medicare and Medicaid were mid-1960s inventions. The numbers of veterans with wartime injuries, both physical and emotional during World War II was in the millions, not thousands. The environment? Coal-fired furnaces were everywhere. Whole cities were covered in clouds of gray smoke and soot. Choose a domestic problem, any problem, and it was worse when they grew up as opposed to those born 50 or 100 years later, at least for now. I know they had it worse than my privileged boomer generation, generation X or today's millennials.

We do face wars and terror but nowhere as horrific as the death and destruction of World War I (when poison gas bombing was commonly used as a weapon), the Armenian Genocide (before Syria even existed as a country), World War II, and the Holocaust. North Korea is not exactly the same nuclear threat the Russians were, especially during the Cuban Missile Crisis of 1962. Refugees refused? How about turning away victims of the Holocaust? Poison gas in Syria? NO comparison to the Nazi poison gas chambers relatives of American families died in. Ask former presidential spokesman Sean Spicer.

Relax. This is not to disparage those in duress today. God knows our world faces too many serious man-made problems. Environmentally, the world may just be slowly coming to an end. We also feel added stress because of the immediacy of media and social media coverage, divisiveness, and fear mongering. But if we take the long historical view of human endeavors, how special is our time? Even the *Jetsons* predicted we would be farther along technologically than we actually are. Where are our flying cars and personal robots? Are we as bad as Orwell's *1984* or Asimov's *Fahrenheit 451* predicted? Nope. We aren't even as bad off as what was "predicted" in *The Man in the High Castle*, Philip K. Dick's alternative history novel and the TV series based on it. All we have is "alternative facts."

There is a monologue in Steven Levenson's new play, *If I Forget*, spoken by the patriarch of the family, Lou Fischer, who in the year 2000, is a 75-year-old World War II veteran. In it he describes the horrors of being one of the American soldiers who liberated Dachau. After a long sigh, he says as I believe Harry would have said, "For you, history is an abstraction, but for us, the ones who survived this century, this long, long, century, there are no abstractions anymore."

Front: Me, grandson Ben, granddaughter Ellie held by granddaughter Lindsay, Allan's first wife Ronnie, Jordan (the bump).
Rear: Jamie, Iris, granddaughter Rudo with an arm draped over "Poppy," Harry, Randolph "Kentuck," Richard, granddaughter Sammie holding mom, and Allan.

ENDNOTES

1 Geraldine Fabrikant, "Revisiting 1917, a Year That Reverberates for Jews Around the World," *New York Times*, March 15, 2017. Retrieved from https://www.nytimes.com/2017/03/15/arts/design/1917-exhibit-world-war-i-jewish-immigration.html

2 Edwin Black, "Eugenics and the Nazis—the California connection," *San Francisco Chronicle*, November 9, 2003.

3 Ilana Abramovitch and Seán Galvin, *Jews of Brooklyn, Waltham*, MA: Brandeis University Press, 2002, p. 5.

4 American-Israeli Cooperative Enterprise (AICE), *Jews in America: The Jewish American Family*.
Retrieved from (http://www.jewishvirtuallibrary.org/jsource/Judaism/usjewfamily.html

5 Ilana Abramovitch and Seán Galvin, *Jews of Brooklyn*, Waltham, MA: Brandeis University Press, 2002, p. 15.

6 Retrieved from https://www.bklynlibrary.org/blog/2013/02/22/nazism-1930s-brooklyn

7 Retrieved from http://www.tenement.org/encyclopedia/ecodepress_greatdepression.htm - collapse

8 "Remembering the Great Depression," *Time*. Retrieved from http://content.time.com/time/specials/packages/article/0,28804,1851306_1851283_1849903,00.html

9 Jeff Kisseloff, *You Must Remember This: An Oral History of Manhattan from the 1890s to World War II*. Baltimore: Johns Hopkins University Press, 1989.

10 Calvin Coolidge, Address to the American Society of Newspaper Editors, Washington, DC, January 17, 1925.

11 "Inwood During the Great Depression," *My Inwood*, March 5, 2010. Retrieved from http://myinwood.net/inwood-during-the-great-depression

12 *The Lexicon*, 1937.

13 The City University of New York, "University History." Retrieved from http://www2.cuny.edu/about/administration/chancellor/university-history/

14 Ibid.

15 Ibid.

16 *The Lexicon,* 1937.

17 E. L. Piesse, *Japan and the Defense of Australia,* 1935, p. 15.

18 Retrieved from http://timesmachine.nytimes.com/timesmachine/1934/12/16/94588399.html?pageNumber=72

19 *New York Times,* December 16, 1934. Retrieved from http://timesmachine.nytimes.com/timesmachine/1934/12/16/94588399.html?pageNumber=72

20 Jim Powell, "The Economic Leadership Secrets of Benito Mussolini," Forbes, February 22, 2012. Retrieved from http://www.cato.org/publications/commentary/economic-leadership-secrets-benito-mussolini

21 Ibid.

22 *New York Times,* February 12, 1933. Retrieved from http://timesmachine.nytimes.com/timesmachine/1933/02/12/issue.html

23 *New York Times,* September 3, 1933. Retrieved from http://timesmachine.nytimes.com/timesmachine/1933/09/03/105800838.html?pageNumber=45

24 United States Holocaust Memorial Museum, "German Foreign Policy 1933–1945," *Holocaust Encyclopedia.* Retrieved from https://www.ushmm.org/wlc/en/article.php?ModuleId=10005203

25 *New York Times,* September 15, 1936. Retrieved from http://timesmachine.nytimes.com/timesmachine/1936/09/15/88695649.html?pageNumber=26

26 Larry Liu, "Economic Policy in Nazi Germany: 1933–1945." *Penn State Review,* October 2013, p. 10.

27 Comments on the July Issue of "Outlook." Retrieved from http://web.archive.org/web/20030812215652/http://www.gsb.com/resource/trust/wmOutlook.html

28 *New York Times,* June 12, 1933. Retrieved from http://timesmachine.nytimes.com/timesmachine/1933/06/12/105391994.html

29 *New York Times,* June 12, 1933. Retrieved from http://timesmachine.nytimes.com/timesmachine/1933/06/12/105391994.html?pageNumber=7

30 *New York Times,* November 16, 1935. Retrieved from (http://timesmachine.nytimes.com/timesmachine/1935/11/16/93501600.html?pageNumber=1)

31 *New York Times,* August 8, 1936, Retrieved from http://timesmachine.nytimes.com/timesmachine/1936/08/08/87973710.html?pageNumber=7

32 United States Holocaust Museum, "Jewish Athletes—Marty Glickman & Sam Stoller." Retrieved from https://www.ushmm.org/exhibition/olympics/?content=jewish_athletes_more

33 "Letters to the Editor," *Ticker,* October 28, 1935. Retrieved from http://ticker.baruch.cuny.edu/files/articles/ticker_19351028.pdf

34 Office of the Historian, "Lend-Lease and Military Aid to the Allies in the Early Years of World War II." Retrieved from https://history.state.gov/milestones/1937-1945/lend-lease

35 "Mayer Kanarek," Geni.com. Retrieved from https://www.geni.com/people/Mayer-Kanarek/6000000008968959846

36 National Archives. Retrieved from http://www.archives.gov/historical-docs/document. html?doc=15

37 "US Army at the Beginning of WW2," WW2 Weapons. Retrieved from http://ww2-weapons.com/us-army-at-the-beginning-of-ww2/

38 United States Coast Guard, "USS *Peterson.*" Retrieved from https://www.uscg. mil/history/webcutters/Peterson.pdf

39 "At Home," *The War.* PBS, September 2007. Retrieved from https://www.pbs.org/ thewar/at_home_war_production.html

40 Richard Stradling, "Temporary Camp Butner Museum to Open Wednesday," *New York Observer,* November 10, 2015. Retrieved from http://www.newsobserver.com/news/ local/article44183193.html#storylink=cpy

41 Sarah Avery, "Love Letters," *The News & Observer*, February 14, 1999.

42 Ibid.

43 Larry King, *Love Letters of World War II.* New York: Crown Publishers, 2001.

44 Sarah Avery, "Love Letters," *The News & Observer*, February 14, 1999.

45 Ibid.

46 Larry King, *Love Letters of World War II.* New York: Crown Publishers, 2001.

47 US Army Field Artillery School, *History of the Field Artillery School, Volume II, World War II*, Fort Sill, OK: Author, October 31, 1946, p. 49. Retrieved from http://www. dtic.mil/dtic/tr/fulltext/u2/a951856.pdf

48 Information regarding the 78th division during World War II is based on these sites: History of the 78th Division—Wikipedia website, 78th Division WW2 Occupation History—US Army website, and *Lightning, The History of the 78th Infantry Division in WWII*—(Divisional Series) by the Division Historical Committee.

49 Sarah Avery, "Love Letters," *The News & Observer*, February 14, 1999.

50 US Army, "78th Infantry Division." Retrieved from http://www.history.army.mil/ documents/eto-ob/78ID-ETO.htm

51 US Army, *Rhineland: The US Army Campaigns of World War II.* Retrieved from http:// www.history.army.mil/brochures/rhineland/rhineland.htm

52 Ibid.

53 Tom MacKnight, Stan Polny, John Binkley, and Ralf Klodt, "78th Division Code Names in WWII," The 78th Division Veteran's Association Lightning Division. "Retrieved from http://www.78thdivision.org/researchNew02.htm

54 Thomas P. Lockhart, Jr. *"Diehard," History of the 309th Infantry Regiment.* Durham, NC: 78th Division Veterans Association. Retrieved from http://www.78thdivision. org/X-Drive/309th/Diehard%20-%20%20History%20of%20the%20309th%20 Infantry%20Regiment.pdf

55 Ibid.

56 John Walker, "Bracketing the Enemy: Forward Observers and Combined Arms Effectiveness During the Second World War," (PhD diss., Kent State University, 2009), pp. 202–204.

57 Ibid, pp. 209–210.

58 John Stanchack, "Book Review: *Soldier from the War Returning: The Greatest Generation's Troubled Homecoming from World War Two*," America in WWII. Retrieved from http://www.americainwwii.com/reviews/soldiers-from-the-war-returning/

59 Ibid.

60 Sarah Avery, "Love Letters," *The News & Observer*, February 14, 1999.

61 Ibid.

62 The Demographic Study Committee of the Federation of Jewish Philanthropies, *Estimated Jewish Population of the New York Area, 1900–1975*. Retrieved from http://www.jewishdatabank.org/studies/downloadFile.cfm?FileID=2523

63 WNET Thirteen, "History of Brooklyn: The Post-War Years," *Brooklyn*. Retrieved from http://www.thirteen.org/brooklyn/history/history5.html

64 United States House of Representatives, "The Permanent Standing House Committee on Un-American Activities," January 3, 1945. Retrieved from http://history.house.gov/Historical-Highlights/1901-1950/The-permanent-standing-House-Committee-on-Un-American-Activities/

65 J. C. Charlet, "Paradise Shot to Hell: The Westbrook Pegler Story," *The Baffler*, December 1999. Retrieved from http://thebaffler.com/salvos/paradise-shot-to-hell-the-westbrook-pegler-story

66 Wendy Wall, "Anti-Communism in the 1950s," The Gilder Lehrman Institute of American History. Retrieved from https://www.gilderlehrman.org/history-by-era/fifties/essays/anti-communism-1950s

67 Irwin Richman, *Borscht Belt Bungalows: Memories of Catskill Summers*. Philadelphia, PA: Temple University Press, 1998. Retrieved from http://www.temple.edu/tempress/chapters_1100/1353_ch1.pdf

68 Jeffrey P. Salkin, "Sixty Years Since the Peekskill Riots," *Forward*, September 2, 2009. Retrieved from http://forward.com/culture/113279/sixty-years-since-the-peekskill-riots/

69 Ibid.

70 Ibid.

71 Ibid.

72 "53c. Land of Television," US History, Retrieved from http://www.ushistory.org/us/53c.asp

73 William Whyte, *The Organization Man*. New York: Simon & Schuster, 1956, p. 10.

74 Ardsley Historical Society, "Ardsley Timeline." Retrieved from http://www.ardsleyhistoricalsociety.org/ardsleytimeline/

75 "50 Best *Mad Men* Characters," *Rolling Stone*. Retrieved from http://www.rollingstone.com/tv/lists/50-best-mad-men-characters-20150511.

76 Andrew Cracknell, *The Real Mad Men*. New York: Running Press, 2011.

77 Larry McShane, "Real New York Executives Fondly Remember the 1960s of *Mad Men*," *New York Daily News*, August 16, 2009. Retrieved from http://www.nydailynews.

com/entertainment/tv-movies/real-new-york-executives-fondly-remember-1960s-mad-men-article-1.400302

78 Lorraine B. Diehl and Marianne Hardart, "The Automat: The History, Recipes, and Allure of Horn & Hardart's Masterpiece." Retrieved from http://www.theautomat.net

79 Norris W. Preyer, "Vick Chemical Company," *Encyclopedia of North Carolina,* ed. William S. Powell. Chapel Hill, NC: University of North Carolina Press, 2006. Retrieved from http://ncpedia.org/vick-chemical-company

80 "Thalidomide," *Chemical & Engineering News.* Retrieved from https://pubs.acs.org/cen/coverstory/83/8325/8325thalidomide.html

81 Robert Norris and Hans M. Kristensen, "Global Nuclear Weapons Inventories, 1945–2010," *Bulletin of the Atomic Scientists,* July 1, 2010. doi: 10.2968/066004008

82 John F. Kennedy, "Report on the Berlin Crisis," July 25, 1961. Retrieved from http://millercenter.org/president/speeches/speech-5740

83 Nikita S. Khrushchev, "Khrushchev's Secret Speech on the Berlin Crisis," August 1961. Retrieved from https://www.mtholyoke.edu/acad/intrel/khrush.htm

84 Allan Sherman, "Hello Muddah, Hello Fadduh (A Letter from Camp)." Retrieved from http://www.oldielyrics.com/lyrics/allan_sherman/hello_muddah_hello_fadduh_a_letter_from_camp.html

85 "So a grocer is restocking the vegetables..." Retrieved from https://www.reddit.com/r/Jokes/comments/1n2rr2/so_a_grocer_is_restocking_the_vegetables/

86 Erica Etelson, *For Our Own Good: The Politics of Parenting in an Ailing Society.* Berkeley, CA: Left Coast Press, 2010.

87 David Ogilvy, *Confessions of an Advertising Man.* London: SouthBank Publishing, 2004.

88 Sheri Carder, "Clio Awards" *The Guide to United States Popular Culture,* ed. Ray B. Browne. Madison, WI: University of Wisconsin Press, 2001, pp. 180–181.

89 David Hack, "Vietnam War Facts, Stats and Myths," US Wings, Retrieved from http://www.uswings.com/about-us-wings/vietnam-war-facts/

90 Federal Reserve Bank of St. Louis, "Economic Research," 2009. Retrieved from https://research.stlouisfed.org

91 Jimmy Carter, "Crisis of Confidence: Energy and National Goals," July 15, 1979. Retrieved from http://www.pbs.org/wgbh/americanexperience/features/primary-resources/carter-crisis/

92 Jody Avirgan, "Why the Bronx Really Burned," FiveThirtyEight, October 29, 2015. Retrieved from http://fivethirtyeight.com/datalab/why-the-bronx-really-burned/

93 Ian Fischer, "Pulling Out of Fort Apache, the Bronx; New 41st Precinct Station House Leaves Behind Symbol of Community's Past Troubles," *New York Times,* June 23, 1993.